NAVIGATING MULTICULTURALISM

GUIDANCE FOR SOCIOLOGICAL CHANGE

HOLLIS L. GREEN

GlobalEdAdvance
Press

NAVIGATING MULTICULTURALISM
Guidance for Sociological Change

Copyright © 2021 by Hollis L. Green
Library of Congress Control Number: 2021903927
ISBN 978-1-950839-10-0
Hollis Lynn Green 1933 -

Subject Codes and Description: 1. SOCIAL SCIENCE/
Sociology/General 2. EDUCATION/Multicultural Education
3. RELIGION/General

Cover by GlobalGraphicsNYC

City of Publication: Nashville, TN

Printed in Australia, Brazil, EU, France, Germany, Italy,
Poland, Russia, Spain, UK, USA and available on the Espresso
Book Machine© worldwide.

Order books from www.gea-books.com/bookstore/
Or any place good books are sold.

Published by
GlobalEdAdvancePRESS
a division of
Global Educational Advance, Inc.
www.GlobalEdAdvance.org

This work is respectfully dedicated to

THE REVEREND DR. JOHN BUUCK

A scholar of the Word and an
Educational leader with a kindred soul
And a missional spirit.

President Emeritus:
Concordia University (Wisconsin)
With a global vision
Launching Universities in
Estonia, Ukraine, Ghana, and Liberia.

Multiculturalism is an ideology that
promotes the institutionalization of
communities containing multiple cultures.
It is applied to the demographic of Post-WWII
communities comprising several cultures.
Related to an educational theory that
diversity is required for a modern society,
the theory is that groups within a society
should maintain cultural difference, but
share overall political and economic power.
It is a philosophical theory that
reality is made up of many kinds of people.

CONTENTS

God wants His Creation back and
all humans filled with faith and love
for their fellowman.

Jesus wants His brand identity back
and prayer restored in His follower's lives.
He desires His rightful place as
Head of the Houses of Worship.

The Spirit is grieved by the lifestyle of
believers as He continues working
to convict the world of sin,
righteousness and judgment.
A Creator God does not dwell in
man-made buildings, but
in the living souls of His disciples.

PREFACE

Accentuate Positive Associations

One humanitarian group will never bring peace or feed the children or care for the sick and dying. One selfless group cannot eliminate poverty, violence, drugs, human trafficking or influence global social change. A priority agenda must be to make people moral citizens of society before they can become mystical citizens of heaven.

The record of early wisdom provides guidance for faith-based groups negotiating constructive change in a multicultural community. Future generations benefit from the logic and common sense of the past: such as, *"one never reaches a positive conclusion beginning with a negative premise"* or "*a positive implies a negative.*" With these two presuppositions one can clearly see the value of common ground and the complications caused by multiple differences. No one can deny the variations of culture, language and tradition which exists in diverse groups. Yet, it is difficult to identify common ground in a multicultural population. Why is this true?

Since a positive implies a negative, *the pro* and *con* of the faith-based Reformation were given a negative connotation. The prefix *pro* is positive and looks forward.

Yes, the Protestant Reformation was viewed as negative by the dominant Universal church, but the objectives were for correcting errors, abuses, and discrepancies. Luther presented a positive basis for salvation as *"the just shall live by faith."* In the environment of grievances, Luther claimed a positive presupposition for a faith-based plan to move worship away from man-made regulations to follow the sacred writings which clearly claimed: *"It is written, Man shall not live by bread alone, but by every word that proceeds out of the mouth of God.* (Matthew 4:4)

Luther published his German NT translation 1522 but posted his theses five years earlier in 1517. It appears to this writer that Luther was working on his German version and may have been translating Hebrews when he proclaimed **"the righteous will live by faith"** by nailing his 95 theses on the door of the castle church in Wittenberg (1517). Perhaps Luther reviewed his translation of Hebrews 10:32-39 which reads something close to what is below. Note the translation of Hebrews 10:32-39 from the German text and the comparison rendering from the Greek text.

GERMAN TO ENGLISH: 32 But remember the days before when, after being enlightened, you endured a great battle of suffering 33 and partly became a spectacle itself through shame and tribulation, partly had fellowship with those who are so concerned. 34 For you have had pity on those who were bound and endured the robbery of your possessions with joy, knowing that with yourselves you have better and lasting possessions in heaven. 35 Do not throw away your trust, which has great rewards. 36 But you need patience, so that you may do the will of God and receive the promise. 37 For "a little while longer," the one who is to come will come, and not pardon. 38 But **the righteous will live by faith,** *but whoever gives way, my soul will not please. 39 We are not of those who give way and are condemned, but of those who believe and save the soul.*

GREEK TO ENGLISH: *32. Remember the hard days, after you had been enlightened and you had to struggle with suffering; 33. there were times when you yourself were exposed to slander and harassment and partly because you came forward to share the suffering of your companions. 34. For you gave sympathy to my bonds, and the seizure of your goods with calm acceptance knowing that in heaven you have better and more material possessions that will endure in heaven. 35.Do not discard compensating self-confidence, for it is a self-reliance that has great reward. 36. For you need steadfastness, after you do the will of God, you must have staying power to receive the promise. 37. Only a brief moment before He who is coming will arrive; He will not linger on the way. 38.* **The justified man lives by faith; but if he withdraws, my soul is not well-pleased. 39. But we are not ones who draw back to destruction; but we are those who accept as true the personal consecration of the mind, will and human emotions which enable us to possess eternal life.**

Many forget they live in a complex environment among groups with different lifestyles and various ancestral backgrounds. This influences groups to cluster with their own kind and creates a mindset of *"us and them."* Then because of social or economic pressure groups become preoccupied with where and how they want to live! Perhaps this is a time when we need to hear someone sing about accentuating the positive.

As a population becomes pluralistic and the dominant culture begins to erode, the culture's harmonizing common elements deteriorate slowly and without effort. As the dominant culture diminishes and the pluralistic aspects of the social order become stronger, the original resistance becomes more heterogeneous and the intent of the founding fathers is over-whelmed by selfish voices seeking control. Order and discipline decline as multiple perspectives clamor for a hearing. The grammar of language suffers, and the meaning of words change, facts of history are lost, and cross-cultural contact fails to arrive on listening ears. Then confusion begins and chaos breeds lawlessness and destruction of property and the tragic death of bystanders become the *"new normal."*

Unfortunately, those who believed they have stormed the Hill of Difficulty and won the battle will suffer greatly without the protection and care of a controlling culture. Only a majority culture can protect minorities as they compete for property, products, and personal safety. Who has the guns? Where are the police? What happened to the government programs? Where are the welfare checks? What happened to the jobs? Why are the faith-based charities and places of worship not assisting the poor? Why has the wealth been moved offshore? Who is collecting the taxes to support public education? Where is government supported healthcare?

These are some unintended consequences of disposing of the rule of law or disrupting the operation of government at any level. This leads to the destruction of family life; although flawed before, it totally fails in the face of chaos in the streets, conflict in the community, corruption, abuse and uncontrolled behavior by elected leaders.

When there is no authority to turn the tide, change the stampede, arrest the criminal element and restore civility to the community, conditions move from bad to worse. Nothing which replaces the common good for all will be better than the pristine order designed by the founders. Those who attempt to *"throw out the baby with the bath water"* * soon learn more about the unintended consequences of their abortive behavior. The children have no secure future, and the family unit continues to deteriorate.

_____

* This expression, with its image of a baby being tossed out with dirty water, is probably translated from a German proverb, *Das Kind mit dem Bade ausschütten."* It was first used in English by Thomas Carlyle (1853).

While attempting to eliminate things which some *"believed to be bad"* other aspects of life which were good are destroyed. Nonviolent protest could awaken elected officials to the needs of their constituent population for a constructive way forward. Yes, there are times when drastic change is required which justifies civil uprising, but this must be a majority decision by the population not the undisciplined voice of an angry mob seeking change for personal benefit without concern for how their actions will work negatively against others. The early words in founding documents speak to these issues.

God, the Father of us all, and our earthly forefathers provided guidance on ways and means to build a country and keep it on the proper path to ensure liberty and justice for all. *"A minority cannot protect itself or other minorities."* Also, it is good policy to "*Correct the inferior before attempting to construct the superior.*" This can only be done by mature and reasonable people. The foundation of justice for all, personal safety, and the general welfare of present and future generations, requires permanent change, not temporary alteration of personal gain.

Foundational documents lose their sense of sacredness and the authority of elected officials decline as multicultural influences increase. There seems to be to many cooks in the community kitchen. Political establishment "*goes along to get along*" with mob rule and the dominant culture is gradually weakened usually without intentional effort and the antecedent structure of a moral society is easily modified. The immorality and hypocrisy of present and past heroes are exposed.

Trusted documents and processes are discarded, and lawless uprisings create rebellion and riot. The destruction of statutes of historic figures which remind the public that things have changed for the better will not change history. However, the process may influence the future: the young will not know the negative aspects of history and may repeat the same behavior which caused the original national upheaval.   Humanity must not be shielded from the tragic aspects of history. A firm hand at the helm and the proper setting of the sails of the Ship of State are required.

Those desiring to influence social change must engage the people in friendly conversation on their home turf. A determined effort to associate freely within the community must be an ongoing endeavor. If change for the better is to come to a community, good people must maintain a friendly presence. Some call this stage of social change a ministry of presence. To complete the process of relationship building, one must create a friendly connection where the outsider is seen as a good and honorable person who has the best interest of others at heart.

The early contacts must not be seen as interlopers working for political advantage, or faith-based do-gooder attempting some charity work. Individuals must see themselves as the beneficiary of something good and valuable to create the atmosphere conducive to friendly exchange of ideas. Friendship may not be the best place to start; in fact, friendship must be earned over time. One cannot listen without clothes, shoes, food, or a place to sleep. Once the process is viewed as a humanitarian effort, a positive presence is established, the normal steps may be taken to make a difference in the community through positive relationship building.

The voice or action of one group will not create positive change; there must be willing cooperation of elected officials and all constituent parties. The wisdom of Solomon is needed to navigate a way forward in a topsy-turvy world. Constructive social change must be a group effort and be seen as a collaborative endeavor that includes the citizens of the community. Academics, clergy, social scientists, sociologists and social researchers are all involved in identifying "best practices" or orthopraxis for sociological change. Psychology deals with individuals, sociology with study groups, and social psychology view individuals as they function within their primary groups. Social researchers use scientific methods appropriate for gathering data relative to a problem. They either seek the "why" it happened or "how" it happened. The "how" leads to the "why" when the interrogatives are engaged: what, why, who, when to arrive at useful answers of how the present condition was initiated. When the "how" is understood and the results are determined, a diagnosis may be made, and a workable plan may be formulated for social change. A collection of this knowledge creates a system of best practices.

> *Sidebar:* Most are familiar with accident investigations to determine "how" and "what" happened. When "how" is determined, the investigator usually understands "why" and "who" were the initiators, and this knowledge is used to construct safety measures to prevent future accidents? Also, a medical autopsy determines, how the person died, then they know the why and the medical community can plan for prevention to avoid such deaths. All these procedures relate to the best practices for community social change.

Hollis L. Green, ThD, PhD, DLitt
Morning Air Estate on Lone Mountain
The Evergreen Cottage
37321-7635 Tennessee USA

January 6, 2021

INTRODUCTION

Orthopraxis for Sociological Change

Social change is any alteration in the cultural,
structural, population, or ecological characteristics
of a social system. In a sense, attention to social
change is inherent in all sociological work
Because social systems are always In the
process of change.

**All communities in a multicultural society are
a mixing bowl of various cultures and traditions.**
Everyone must assist constructive social progress. Each
opening for positive change requires action. There are
occasions in most communities to produce positive
change and moral progress; therefore, it becomes an
obligation for all concerned to work toward such social
advance and transformation of their community. This is
particularly incumbent on community leadership to see
that the mixing bowl does not become a simmering stew
pot of festering frustration.

Social Change is an essential resource for the entire
spectrum of social life. Some make good connections
with inspiring friends and colleagues, from people who
are just entering public life to seasoned veterans of
human struggles -- and leave every event recharged and
excited to make a positive impact on the world.

Social change agents and groups make extraordinary things happen. These alterations are characterized by changes such as rules of behavior, values, social organizations and cultural symbols. The term "social change" describes a significant alteration that sociologists describe as changes that result in extraordinary human consequences.

Social change uses the term change as a broad umbrella to encompass a range of typical social and community outcomes from increased awareness and understanding, to attitudinal change, to increased local participation, the building of public good will, to policy change that corrects injustice.

Social change, in its broadest meaning, is defined by any change to a society as a whole. It follows the idea that society is a constantly changing unit and the perpetual movement must be channeled in a constructive direction that improves behavior, reinforces ethics and values, maintains moral standards and works for fairness and equality among all people in all organizations, institutions and government operations. The goal is a collaborative work to make the social order a fairer, more inclusive and moral society.

Some change may require the acceptance of mixing of few community traditions and cultures. By adding some aspect of one culture to another, the assimilation produces common ground for constructive change. The combination of traditions produces transformation and adjustments to both thought and process. As change is assimilated, answers are worked out in advance for anticipated questions and a positive attitude for interaction becomes a way of life. This tactic produces a strategy for positive change as individuals adjust to the differences around them. The ability to accommodate and adjust to a changing environment or accept a larger association is a noble and valued aspect of human existence. In fact, this is what makes the world go around or at least move forward toward common ground known as progress in a civil society.

There are as many approaches to social change as there are individuals. As individuals function within a given culture or tradition, they constantly seek both intellectual and behavioral improvement. There is an automatic reaching for a new and better way and an ambitious striving toward different and higher goals. The restraining forces which obstruct such progress must be identified and seriously considered.

The restraints that prevent progress come in the forms of personal identity, language, religion and cultural traditions. Certain aspects of culture: food, clothing, music, politics, family life and personal and social distance normally do not cause difficulty. As one matures in social graces, they become willing to overlook traditional and cultural warnings and navigate or negotiate both social and personal aspects of their life to better understand their neighbors. It is this course of action that facilitates constructive social change in almost every aspect of life except religion.

In the process of social change there is concern that one does not become tainted by the moral deficiencies of another culture, tradition or individual behavior. It is in this regard that one must be vigilant, willing to take a cautious look at other cultures and faith-based traditions, but to also be discerning and accept only those aspects of another culture or tradition that does not violate the personal moral standard of expected behavior. The intention is to allow good to overcome evil rather than to sanction immoral conduct. Should one accept the dishonorable aspects of a culture or tradition and attempt to imitate shameful behavior, a progressive debauchery quickly establishes a slippery slope toward evil that produces a deterioration in the moral values and meaningful traditions of the community. In such cases no one wins, and everyone loses!

All citizens must be on guard against moral decline that ultimately blocks all constructive change. The process of integration is designed to make whole or new by adding or bringing together different parts. The study of faith-based thinking is any cultural system which directs people to the supernatural or worship of a Higher Power. At the level of ideology ideas and values are produced that enables different individuals and divergent groups to find common ground and accept incremental constructive change.

This takes place as a formation in the affective domain where ideas of an individual or group are derived exclusively through feelings. Philosophy is the basic awareness of knowledge, reality, and existence which enables one to develop a personal identity which determines social roles and the function of individuals in families, groups and other organizations tied to the culture.

Since feelings can be deceptive, the affective domain must be balanced with the processes governing thought and conduct including aesthetics, ethics, logic, meta-physics, morals, faith, character and behavior.

This combined with faith-based living that considers the relationship between the Divine and the universe as to matters of lifestyle behavior is a good place to be. Consequently, one must be aware that all aspects of sociological integration and personal change are emotional and may be disturbing and at times troubling. However, the need for social progress and moral development demands that efforts be made to advance community constructive social change.

The goals of this work are:

1. Establish a rationale for sociological contextualization.
2. Value the various spheres of human life and culture.
3. View faith-based operations in cultural clothes
4. Distinguish between theology and ideology
5. Develop a needs fulfillment in group interaction.
6. See how human needs (psychological, moral, social, and intellectual) are fulfilled by social connectedness.
7. Discover how moral nurturing can narrow contact with non-compliant elements of a community and hinder personal development and sociological integration of human effort to formulate and enlarge a faith-based lifestyle.

Constructive social change does not come easily. Both behavior and faith-based reasoning are modified over time as social interactions increase. When the people are viewed as a whole one sees a different picture than when the community is broken down into parts. Cultures, traditions, ethnic groups, business organizations, government personnel, religious institutions, social clubs, medical facilities, and institutions of learning all function in response to current behavior and intellectual reasoning. Separating a whole into parts assists leaders in determining the nature, proportion, function, and relationship of various aspects of the community in order to weave or knit together a new integrated entity that would demonstrate constructive social progress.

A minority cannot protect itself from the violence imposed by discrimination, injustice, or prejudice. Community leaders must make a contextual analysis of the population by looking at every aspect of the community. When choices are made on the basis of gender, race, religion, ethnic origin or lifestyle behavior rather than on core values and character, little can be done without external forces coming to the rescue. Internal resistance only breeds more expressions of violence and prejudicial behavior. The situation gets worse!

Only a willing majority can honestly negotiate from strength and make small progressive steps to facilitate constructive change. This is not done by laws, but by clear rejection of negative behavior on both sides of the issue and an honest adjustment of attitude. What is needed is not only affirmative action, but an affirmative attitude, a predisposition to act positively in each situation. Everyone must be seen as a person of worth with a potential productive contribution to the community. Even bad behavior can become a "good bad example" to others. Without this attitude, positive social change will be greatly hindered.

Civil Rights Laws and affirmative action made a small difference for some at the level of overt discrimination and injustice, but not in the core attitude of the majority. There are still those in the majority that either accept the whole and reject the part or accept the part and reject the whole. What is needed is an affirmative attitude toward all people. The articulation of an assenting approach to responsible change, lawful behavior, and the attitude of a good neighbor should come from a positive predisposition to behave responsibly in all human interaction.

Normally, a population will accept a minority, an ethnic group, or a social class into the community to the degree the group exists on the national scene. Since people gather in groups according to cultural orientation: food selection, clothing style, music appreciation, spoken language, family religion, political choice, and ethnic background, different groups must be viewed based on their function in the community. When a single group grows beyond the national norm in a given community, others begin to show favoritism or express prejudice. It is a natural observable circumstance and a warning sign that social progress is slowing down, and bias and prejudice are evident and expressed.

This discrimination at first is a natural occurrence, but as crime, loss of jobs, and negative personal encounters increase more disapproving feelings are expressed. It then begins to take on a life of its own and grows exponentially until violence beaks out. Laws, housing and school zoning, highway and street constructions or similar efforts to fence in a minority cannot stop the growing feelings of resentment.

Prejudice, bigotry, and narrow mindedness are normally learned in the home, not on the streets. Prejudice is normally taught by example in the family or caught in the unruly streets.

The family unit is the key to understanding discrimination and should never be undervalued. It would be good if everyone could accept the family across the street as part of the community. It would be great if whole families could communicate and build unbiased relationships with others as the younger children do. Could sacred writings have the answer: *"Unless you change and become as little children, you will never enter heaven."* (Matthew 18:3) It appears that the Afterlife is connected to the present Lifestyle behavior.

This level of communication will not happen until there is an internal redirection of attitudes at home; it will not take place until parents and older siblings behave responsibly and become examples of moral citizens. However, individuals cannot change by themselves. Normally, it takes an outside push such as, religion, community recreation, political fairness, or just plain good and moral parenting to affect such change. It may take a drastic readjustment of the *psyche* or inner self to make a major adjustment to the subconscious attitude and generate a willingness to behave as a moral citizen of the community. Such a transition is a high achievement of basic human interaction working with divine intervention. When this occurs, others are influenced to move in a positive direction. Social change begins with one and spreads to others. It is a process.

Everyone is in a hurry to make constructive changes, but reality must be faced squarely. Haste makes waste.

It takes as long to solve a social problem as it took to create the problem in the first place. To establish a new habit or routine it takes as many as twenty-one (21) consecutive efforts, and one default returns the count to a restart. This is why it is difficult to make a change in habitual behavior. Such effort must be practiced habitually before becoming a lifestyle trait.

Some gender, racial, ethnic, religious, and national origin issues have been with society for many years. Does this mean constructive change can never happen? Of course, not! However, understanding the social change theory does assist the appreciation for the small change becoming as one sees and increases the tolerance for the gradual improvements that take place. Is the change moving fast enough? Of course, not! Again, the process can be nudged a little, but it cannot be pushed beyond the norms of a change timetable unless a spiritual element impacts the process.

A traumatic event is a wound to the cognitive or emotional state of a person that may cause prolonged or extended change of lifestyle and behavior. Trauma may be either/or negative or positive. When a young child is molested or a young girl is raped, the long-term improvement depends on the positive or negative attitude of the caregiver or treatment. If the incident is permitted to become a life-changing event it may go in either direction. Provided a victim of incest or rape is treated as "*it **was** or **was not** your fault*" the outcome is obvious. In cases of incest, rape or physical mistreatment, provided a caregiver is capable of treating trauma as a life-changing rather than a life-threating event, a positive outcome is possible. In the above cases, if the treatment is only physical with no emotional management there may be negative trauma without the sensitive care required for positive life-changing trauma.

[*This effort is not guidance for treatment, but an effort to show that positive or negative input will produce the corresponding outcome: positive = positive, negative = negative. This is validated by the "proportional to" provision in math which uses the symbol of a stretched-out* **alpha** *which resembles a* **fish**.]

α *A stretched-out* **alpha** *appears to be a* **fish**

Part of the problem is that minority groups have raised their expectations beyond the limits of normal social change. Also, some of the majority have either stuck their heads in the sand or dug their heels in the dirt. Higher levels of change would require a drastic and costly revolution such as historic civil hostilities. Tolerance must be taught, demonstrated, and lived daily in the community to prepare for constructive social progress.

Discrimination must be condemned and corrected. Honesty and fairness must control all relationships. Then, and only then, can people in a multicultural community live in peace and comfort with neighbors at the family table, next door or across the street. It may be slow coming; be patient.

Patience is a virtue in all aspects of life. It is the ability to remain under pressure of the situation with a positive attitude until constructive change comes. That is why the Ancient Greeks called the sick who came to see a physician "patients," because they had to remain under the pressure of illness until the practitioner was able to treat their infirmity. Patience means a calm endurance of hardship, inconvenience or delay until better conditions happen.

Patience is identified by tolerance of a situation that is less than acceptable; it is developed by hardship and misfortune and strengthened by enduring the present, magnified by uncomplaining hope, and characterized by a forgiving spirit directed toward an antecedent cause or those who openly resist change. This requires transparency in relationships.

Significant faith begins with the
integrity of a founder. Early faith-based
leaders were admired for truthfulness
and reliability. Followers believed in the
person's steadfastness before they could
accept their reliability. History verifies
a leader's words are worthless without the
acceptance of followers. Early disciples
were not asked about belief,
The Master asked, "Who am I?"

Chapter One

AUTHENTICATE

A RELEVANT FAITH

Wisdom is the ability to integrate relevant information and use it wisely. This commonsense grounding for early followers was both an attraction to the leader's nobility and acceptance of their personal integrity in communicating with the people. This is what Luke, the only Gentile writer of the New Testament, shared the gospel with Theophilus in Rome that he and his friends worshiped a God who became a man, and His name was Jesus. He then compared Rome's adoration and worship of Caesar, a man who claimed to be a god. The Romans called their man/god Caesar; Luke was clear that he worshipped a God/man known as Jesus.

Luke overwhelmingly used "Jesus" instead of "Christ" permitting others to use the Messiah reference. Why? The Jewish population looked for a "Messiah", but Luke presented the Roman society a Godly Warrior who willingly took on the Evil One and gave His life for the rescue of humanity. Caesar or the god/Idols of Rome could not promise redemption to citizens of the Empire much less to the entire human race. Luke in his professional understanding was sharing the Jesus was part of the human race and understood the earthly trials and difficulties of humanity. So called gods living in a palace using the wealth of the people to wage war to gain more riches is an interloper and trespasser without power to save the people from butchery of enemy slaughter.

Luke made it clear that Jesus, an emergent leader was also a teacher who attracted learners who attached themselves to the teacher to gain intimate knowledge of a new way of life. Their fellowship became a discipleship to learn *"all that Jesus began to do and teach."* As a master teacher, this Jesus, continuously taught and often repeating basic truths to be sure they were understood. From the study of eye-witness accounts, Luke was convinced that the past details had present value to the pagan Greco-Roman Empire. It appears that Luke gathered basic information to guide the early Gentile believers along their journey to become moral citizens of the world and be welcomed as mystical citizens of heaven.

As a professional and a scholar, Luke understood that many original facts would be overlooked or neglected by future faith-based people. His two-volume work was an effort to draw attention to historical facts which still speak truth to power for believers as they enter the straight and narrow way that leads to life eternal. Even though Luke demonstrated great academic skill in presenting his Gospel record and the early history of spiritual leaders in the Acts of The Apostles, the "inspiration" of Luke's work has not been challenged by historical records or serious academics

> 9. *The Lord is not slow concerning His promise as some count slowness; but is longsuffering to all,*

*not wishing any to perish, but desiring all to take
the way of repentance.* (2 Peter 3:9)

Aware of emphasis by position and proportion,
this writer sees Luke's Gospel and the Acts that
covers about one-fourth of the New Testament about
the same proportion as Paul's writings. Luke's ethnic
and professional background provides an academic
excellence in Greek not seen in much of the writing of his
day. Luke was not an eyewitness to the events recorded
in his Gospel, but Luke 1:1-4 describes his research
skills and he presented significant details others omitted.
Since Luke was a Gentile physician, he was concerned
with Jesus' ability to heal and perform other miracles
which clearly made individuals able to follow Him and His
guidance.

Luke intended to write a message that would
convince the Greco-Roman culture and pagan religion
that the claims of Jesus were valid. He addressed
the message to the most excellent Theophilus, a title
normally left for a high Roman official class. Luke's
Gospel was to the Gentiles, presented in a universal
manner with no concern for the Hebrew traditions. He
dealt with prayer, women, praise and historical facts in a
manner unlike other writers of scripture and he used the
best Greek in the New Testament.

[Some are not aware that upper class Romans were also
taught Greek and that Jewish families scattered in the empire
hired Greek slaves to teach Greek to their children.]

Since Luke's first volume, the Gospel, was about
foundational teachings presented to early followers.
These learners became the dedicated messengers
demonstrating both attitude and action of the pristine

faith-based believers empowered by the Holy Spirit and the challenge of Jesus to His followers. Would it not be great if faith-based leadership would say "YES" and agree with God's AMEN and do His will and follow His way?

> I'll say yes, Lord, yes
> To your will and to your way.
> I'll say yes, Lord, yes
> I will trust you and obey.
> When your Spirit speaks to me,
> With my whole heart I'll agree,
> And my answer will be yes, Lord, yes.

—Lyrics by Shirley Caesar

18. And Jesus came and spoke, saying, all authority has been committed to Me in heaven and in earth. 19. *As you personally go, (going) therefore, and make disciples of all nations, baptizing them in the name of the Father, and of the Son, and of the Holy Spirit: 20. teaching them to observe all things whatever I have commanded you: and behold, I am with you* always, even unto the end of the world. Amen. (Mathew 28:18-20 EDNT)

Luke's two volumes provides a clear historical view of how the followers of *"the way"* navigated their journey through the maze of multicultural distractions and persecutions to establish a workable lifestyle for early converts. For this reason, the lessons to be learned from Luke's writings are vital to a clear understanding of the principles upon which faith-based living was founded and the constructs that should guide present believers in prayer and worship. Judaism, Christianity and Islam make consistent prayer a vital part of believer's lifestyle.

All the Monotheistic Religions Include prayer to One God in their system of practices for the faithful. Prayer is an essential part of a Relevant Faith.

The Prayer of the Chalice was used in the Chapel and other academic functions as an "element-less communion" connected with morning prayers. For decades, devotional readings were read in a language other than English to accommodate a pluralistic student body.

A tradition initiated by **Spiros Zodhiates, ThD** whose mother tongue was Greek.

PRAYER OF THE CHALICE

ENGLISH

CREATOR GOD, to Thee I raise my whole being
~a vessel emptied of self. Accept,
this my emptiness and so fill me with
Thyself ~ Thy Light, Thy Love, Thy life -
that these Thy precious Gifts may
radiate through me and overflow
the chalice of my heart into
the hearts of all with whom I
come in contact this day
revealing unto them
the beauty of
Thy Joy and
Wholeness
and
the
serenity
of Thy Peace
which nothing can destroy.

HEBREW

תפילה של הגביע

אלוהים יוצר, אלייך אני מגדל את כל ישותי

כלי מרוקן מעצמי. קבל זאת ~

זה הריקנות שלי וכך למלא אותי עם

את עצמך ~ האור שלך, האהבה שלך, החיים שלך -

שהמתנות היקרות האלה שלך עשויות

מקרינים דרכי ומוצפים

את גביע ליבי אל

את ליבם של כולם שאיתם אני

לבוא במגע היום

מגלה להם

היופי של

השמחה שלך

וּ שְׁלֵמוּת

ה ו

רוֹגַע

לשלום שלך

ששום דבר לא יכול להרוס

GREEK

ΥΠΕΥΘΥΝΟΣ ΤΗΣ ΑΣΚΗΣΗΣ

ΔΗΜΙΟΥΡΓΙΚΟΣ ΘΕΟΣ, για σένα υψώνω ολόκληρη την ύπαρξή μου

~ ένα σκάφος που αδειάζει από τον εαυτό του. Αποδέχομαι,

αυτό το κενό μου και έτσι γεμίστε με

Ο εαυτός σου ~ Το φως σου, η αγάπη σου, η ζωή σου -

ότι αυτά τα πολύτιμα δώρα Σου μπορούν

ακτινοβολεί μέσα μου και ξεχειλίζει

στον δισκοπότηρο της καρδιάς μου

τις καρδιές όλων με τους οποίους εγώ

ελάτε σε επαφή σήμερα

αποκαλύπτοντάς τους

η ομορφιά του

Η χαρά σου και

Ολότητα

και

ο

ηρεμία

της Ειρήνης Σου

που τίποτα δεν μπορεί να καταστρέψει.

ARABIC

صلاة التحدي

أيها الخالق ، إلي أن أ كيك أرفع كياني بالكامل

~ إن انإ ءلاخ يلي من النفس. ق قبول،

اذه فرارغي ألمني به

نفسك ~ نورك ، حبك ، حياتك -

هذه الهدايا الثمينة الخاصة بك

تشع من خلالي وتفيض

كأس قلبي

قلوب جميع الذين انا معهم

تعال على اتصال اذه هذا اليوم

كاشفة لهم

جمال

فرحتك و

الكمال

و

ال

راحة نفسية

سلامك

ردمر. ال شيء يمكن أن يدمر.

SPANISH

ORACIÓN DEL CÁLIZ

DIOS CREADOR, a Ti levanto todo mi ser

~ un recipiente vaciado de sí mismo. Acepta

Esto este mi vacio y asi lléname de Tú mismo

~ Tu Luz, Tu Amor, Tu vida –para que estos

Tus preciosos dones irradiar a través de mí

y desbordar el cáliz de mi corazón en

los corazones de todos con quienes

yo entrar en contacto este día

revelándoles

la belleza de

Tu alegría y

Integridad

y la

serenidad

de tu

paz

que nada puede destruir

GERMAN

GEBET DER CHALICE

SCHÖPFER GOTT, zu Dir erhebe ich mein ganzes Wesen

~ Ein Gefäß, das von sich selbst entleert ist. Akzeptieren,

das ist meine Leere und so fülle mich mit

Du selbst ~ Dein Licht, Deine Liebe, Dein Leben -

damit diese Deine kostbaren Gaben mögen

durch mich strahlen und überlaufen

der Kelch meines Herzens in

die Herzen aller, mit denen ich

Komm heute in Kontakt

ihnen offenbaren

die Schönheit von

Deine Freude und

Ganzheit

und

das

Gelassenheit

deines Friedens

was nichts zerstören kann.

Chapter Two

APPLY
CURATIVE PRAYER NOT PALLIATIVE CARE

*Wellness is not the absence of pain,
sickness is not the end of life and
Palliative care may be the denial of hope.
There is a place for end-of-life comfort,
but God is in charge of life and death.
Pain and grief are part of being human
and illness is an intimate part of life.
Personal assurance of an afterlife
can produce a hopeful lifestyle
worthy of the journey!*

How does one proceed with constructive change in a multicultural community? Focus on the known concerns at hand; do not waste your prayer time just to feel good about something. At times zero has meaning, such as, the absence of oxygen, water, food, clothing, shelter, safety, love and family. Certainly, one who prays will feel better, but that is not the objective. Prayerfully trusting God in the critical circumstances of life is a process with great curative value. Since prayer from a believing heart is both restorative and productive, why is

prayer so frequently neglected? Since a sincere appeal
to a Higher Power is the place to start on the journey
back to God's promised provisions, why do we overlook
the power of prayer? God listens to the prayers within
the parameters of His Will.

> *Ask and you shall receive, seek and you will find,*
> *knock and faith will open the door from the inside.*
> (Luke 11:9-10)

> 14. **And this is the freedom that we have to**
> **approach God that He listens when we ask**
> **anything according to His** w*ill. 15. And if we*
> *know He listens to us, whatsoever we ask, we*
> *know we have the requests made to Him.* (I John
> 5:14-15 EDNT)

One summer in VBS, the children were singing, "If
you are *saved* and you know it, say AMEN!" One young
girl was boldly singing, "If you are *SAFE,* etc." The
teacher attempted to correct her, but with no success.
Her brother was a star on a Little League Team, and
she understood being "**safe on base.**" She had never
been lost in the woods or drowning in the river and did
not understand the concept of being "saved" but clearly
understood being "safe."

Later while preparing a sermon, it was discovered
the word "**saved**" meant "***to make safe.***" Perhaps the
child was correct; she was happy because she felt "safe."
From the mouth of a child came a lesson learned, not in
Sunday school, church or a Bible class, but learned in
a Little League game. Sports participation has special
value for the younger siblings of those who diligently play
by the rules of the game.

In the case of social and/or spiritual change in a multicultural community, there are procedures and rules which must be followed. In the realm of family and religion, prayer is an essential element of the process for constructive change. After parents and friends have done all they can do to bring about improved behavior, in the final analysis God must intervene. The sincere desire of the heart expressed in thought or word becomes a spiritual invitation for divine intervention.

When realistic faith issues from deep within the heart and soul, positive guidance will be forthcoming. God always listens to the spoken and unspoken words from a seeking heart. When the prayer is heard, the answer will be "Yes, No, or Later" but prayer with unwavering faith always receives an answer! Any anticipated positive change in a group or community must begin with the practice of consistent and persistent appeal for divine assistance to enable constructive change in the lives of individuals.

Daniel had no time for calming or soothing prayer, it was a life- or-death matter and a comfortable placebo prayer was not sufficient. It was time for an effectual, fervent and curative prayer with earnest expectation of a timely answer. Daniel and his friends were facing serious difficulty. Daniel and the Hebrew children experienced God's swift answer before and during dangerous times: just in time to drastically change uncertain situations. Daniel was facing a precarious set of circumstances. No time for a "now I lay me down to sleep; I pray the Lord my soul to keep. If I should die before I wake, I pray the Lord my soul to take. Examine Daniel's prayer (Daniel 9:20-21) from **a candid rendering of the Hebrew text. ***

*20 While I was arranging words to pray and
seeking God for answers in weakness reaching
for God's Hand in an overwhelming situation
entreating for mercy and grace. 21 And while I
was arranging words to seek God a divine hand
touched me about the time of my voluntary gift as
part of worship.

Note the rendering of bold words: *20. While
I was **speaking** (arranging words to pray)
and **praying** (seeking God for answers) and
confessing (in weakness reaching for God's
Hand) **presenting** (in an overwhelming situation)
my **supplication** (entreating for mercy and
grace). 21. While I was **speaking in prayer** I was
touched (a divine hand was placed on me) about
the time of my **oblation** (voluntary gift as part of
worship).

Curative prayer is personal and purifying coming
from a sincere heart. Confession is good for the soul and
has a cleansing result which establishes communion with
God and opens the door to worship and the "washing
of the soul." Prayer from the heart is a positive petition
to God for a personal and specific issue. True prayer
occurs when a person has a personal stake in the
outcome; this happens when one prays for someone or
something that is connected to the circumstance of their
own life. What could we learn from a Boolean search
strategy for data retrieval based on the words used to
spell **h-e-a-r-t?** There are three words: "art," "ear" and
"hear." What can be learned from the defining of each
word when the combined meaning yields the identity or
value of the whole structure of a word.

The heart of the matter contains the subjective
ability to understand when sensitive listening assesses

the core meaning of each part which yields the functional value of the whole construct: *h-e-a-r-t.*

> *45. A good man produces a good treasure from his heart; and an evil man produces plunder that is evil: for from the abundance of the heart the mouth speaks.* (Luke 6:45 EDNT)

Prayer changes people and people change things; however, a short-cut is often taken which declares **"Prayer changes things!"** This idea weakens prayer and causes a misdirection of spiritual concern. Take a look at the two premises of the syllogism and the conclusion:

Premise One: *People have problems.*

Premise Two: *Prayer changes people.*

Conclusion: *Prayer changes people and people change problems.*

The structure of 'prayer" was in the Greek Middle Voice at least a dozen times in the New Testament. The Middle Voice is selfish and suggests a personal stake in the outcome.

> *"Where two or three are gathered in My Name and pray whatsoever they ask* (for themselves) *will be answered."* (Matthew 18:19,20)

An unspoken question, *"When did parents begin to pray for their children."* It appears from the Genesis record after Cain killed Abel and Adam and Eve had another son called *Seth* who was appointed as a *substitute* for Abel. Then in the course of time, Seth produced a son called, *Enosh,* meaning *mortal.* Since cold-blooded murder and corrupt worship had entered the family and now the legacy of a grandson, the Bible is clear *". then began men to call upon the name of the Lord." (*Genesis 4:24—26 KJV).

Enosh, was Adam's first grandson and since God's command was to be *"fruitful and replenish the earth,"* cold-blooded murder and false worship had complicated family life, it became obvious that grandparents realized they needed moral and spiritual guidance to enable the next generation to have a better life. With the birth of the first grandchild there was a nurturing instinct which naturally developed in the mind, heart and soul of relatives. In an effort to develop a Together-Strong Network to bring about constructive change in a multicultural community one must first look for mature individuals with the life-experience of parenting. This would mean an effort to identify and recruit both mature men and women who have demonstrated love and concern for children, their own and those of others. Nothing in the human experience prepares one to seek a better life for the next generation than the birth of a child in the family.

It is obvious that caring for children seems to develop a special DNA = Divine Nurturing Attribute. This is supported by the sacred writings of Paul in 1 Thessalonians and Galatians, when he explained his behavior as a "mother" and a "father.":

> *7. But we were* **tender among you, <u>even as a nursing mother warmly takes pleasure in her children: 8.</u> so affectionately longing for you, we were willing to share with you, not only the gospel of God, but also well-pleased to share our lives, because you were valued by us.**
> *9. You remember our long and hard labor night and day, because we would not burden you for*

expenses, but freely preached the gospel of God unto you. **10. You are witnesses and so is God, how upright, honest and blameless was our conduct among you that believe: 11. as you know how we <u>encouraged, comforted, and charged every one of you, as a father treats his children</u>, 12. that you would lead a life worthy of God,** (1 Thessalonians 2:7-12 EDNT)

19. **You are my little children and I have a mother's birth pains** *again until Christ is formed in you, 20. I stand in uncertainty about you and wish I could be present with you and speak to you in a more pleasant tone. (*Galatians 4:19,20 EDNT)

It was genuine delight to discover my name written in the margin of my grandfather's Bible. He had a custom of reading five (5) chapters during each day. He would write in the margin the names of those who came to mind or came by his place during the day. In his evening prayers, he would pray for the people whose names appeared in the margin of the passages he had read that day. It was a great joy to discover my name many times in the margin of Grandfather's Bible and to realize he had regularly prayed for me.

Grandfather's effort to teach me the lessons of life after my father died became a central part my being today. God give us more good parents and grandparents! They are desperately needed to keep the next generation on the straight and narrow way. I personally discovered it was difficult to be too broadminded and walk the narrow way that leads to life eternal. After all, it is the eternal things that really count, now and forever. Grandfather's prayers joined with Mother's prayers became a fence on both sides of the road that kept me on the straight path toward Heaven.

Intercessory prayer is personal, positive, particular, and self-purifying. At least a dozen times in the New Testament the Greek Middle Voice, which has a selfish connotation, is used in relationship with prayer. One must have a personal stake in the outcome of prayer for the words to come from the heart. *"Whatsoever you ask (for yourself.)" Parents and grandparents have much at stake with the future of their children and grandchildren.* For this reason, mature parents and grandparents are the most effective persons to recruit into a community "Together/Strong" NETWORK to pray and work for positive social and spiritual change in a multicultural community.

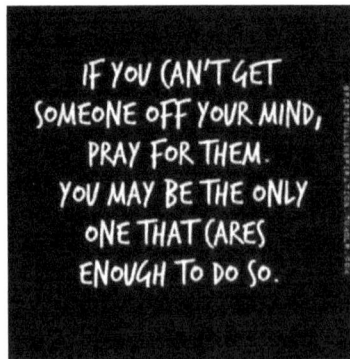

IF YOU CAN'T GET
SOMEONE OFF YOUR MIND,
PRAY FOR THEM.
YOU MAY BE THE ONLY
ONE THAT CARES
ENOUGH TO DO SO.

SpiritualInspiration.tumblr

Some years ago, the "Pray for Pedro" program was shared with a church in St. Croix, USVI. The topic was intercessory prayer that one could not pray for others without receiving a blessing themselves. At the close of a Sunday through Wednesday meeting a young girl, about 10, wrote me a note: *"Dear Dr. Green, I like your preaching. I like stories about people's lives. I enjoyed Mrs. Green's singing; it was warm and soft* *and comfortable.* **And prayer is just like jam. You can't spread even a little without getting some on yourself.** *"* *[Children do understand the message!]

Since communities are the creation of human beings, they are flawed. There are no perfect neighborhoods, townships or cities, the grass is always greener on the other side of the hedge row. Yet, reality teaches us that weeds grow with the grass and even take over the unused pathways. An old proverb speaks directly to the idea of maintaining friendship: *"Go often to the house of your friends for weeds soon choke an unused path."* There is a scriptural construct in Proverbs which validates this: *"One who would have friends must first show himself to be friendly."* The word *friend* prompts several relational words: *association, colleague, companion, contact, well-wisher, and workmate.* Keep in touch with all acquaintances both friend and foe.

Faith-based people are instructed to *"Love their enemies and pray for those who despitefully use them."* How can this be done? Start with genuine forgiveness then focus on the good qualities of the estranged one. Think good thoughts and speak well of them to others. Discover what you have in common with the person or group and embrace the sameness. Common ground can be a good place to stand and walk the path toward reconciliation.

Charity is not the answer but sharing what you have is the end of the beginning that leads to improved friendships and reconciliation with foes. All of the above will cause one to step out of their comfort zone and associate freely with others sharing good news and good words. Peter, the rough talking temperamental fisherman, wrote about kind words:

> 9. *you must not repay injury with injury, or hard words with hard words, but bless those who curse you.* **For you were called to give kind words to others and come to a well-spoken eulogy at the end.** (1 Peter 3:9 EDNT)

Most remember the wisdom of Abraham Lincoln, but recently I found a Lincoln answer to a question about destroying an enemy: *"The best way to destroy an enemy is to make him a friend."* However, I would replace the word "destroy" with "change." *Destroy* appears to be negative and out of character for the Great Emancipator. Lincoln in dealing with the sorrows of the Civil War in his Second Inaugural said, *"with malice toward none, with charity for all."* I would change "destroy" to "change, transform, or replace." These seem to better fit my image of Lincoln. At times a poorly asked question may receive a flawed answer. Hopefully, this was the case with Lincoln's use of *destroy.*

Faith-based individuals with a moral lifestyle should view adversarial conflict from a positive perspective. With each such conflict there is a way to navigate a pathway to a corrective solution. Always find a way to express concern in a positive way. In this same manner when considering another's negative participation, instead of "absent" the word "away" comes to mind. Friends and loved ones are never absent, only away. Family and friends who have passed on remain "loved ones" and they are just "away." Life goes forward and never stands still: the word *absent* is permanently negative!

How can a loved one be *absent* when they *march through your memory and parade through your dreams?* They are embedded in your subconscious memory, part of your decision-making process and remain deep within your emotional realty. Loved ones are not absent but are in the Arms of a Loving God and part of a "cloud of witnesses" who encourage us to rid ourselves of all that could hinder the course that leads to the great reunion in Heaven. (Hebrews 12:1-2)

As a Graduate Professor, when a good student missed class it was presumed to be unavoidable and he/she was marked "away." As a pastor, when a faithful member was not present at worship, it was assumed they were on a divine mission to share the message of love and grace with those not able to attend. We must put emphasis on the positive to make progress. This not only keeps the weeds out of the path but also the briars and thorns cut out of relationships. It would be good to remember the roadway to the Cities of Refuge in the Old Testament were straight and kept clear of all barriers to those seeking shelter and protection from revenge and retribution.

Transparency must be clear to all
Participants in any alliance, partnership,
coalition or relationship. Unless such
openness is maintained, progress will
be stifled and conditions will remain
unacceptable. When progress is stopped,
the restart is more difficult.

Chapter Three

ASSURE
TRANSPARENCY IN RELATIONSHIPS

There must be observable openness in association and dealings with multicultural groups. Any hidden agenda will block cooperation even in areas of mutual concern. No constructive change will occur without clear and full comprehension of the initiator's motives. All action must be seen as beneficial to the individuals and families of the community. All compromise must be seen as the *promise* of mutual advancement for all.

> *26. If any man among you seem to be devout, and restrains not his unnatural language, he deceives his own heart and his service to God is ineffective. 27. Free from all that would dim the transparency in belief and conduct before God and the Father is this, to go see and relieve the orphans without a father's protection and the women lacking a husband in their distress, and to keep himself untainted with guilt. (James 1:26-27 EDNT)*

Those who would initiate change must have a clear understanding of the background of the groups involved. All suggested or proposed change must be dealt with in light of the cultural glue which holds groups and their traditional behaviors together. Only then can progress be made in small increments. Drastic or rapid change may destroy all hope for incremental changes that must occur over time. Change advocates must remain patient and approachable by all who have fresh ideas to support positive movement toward constructive change. All who seek change must be willing to be changed themselves. Unless there is an obvious willingness for mutual change, the process will become regressive and the pendulum will swing backward. Usually when the pendulum moves it swings back past the beginning point.

In understanding the nature of the people involved, one must know the values and viewpoint of their group and their faith-based system of religious conviction.

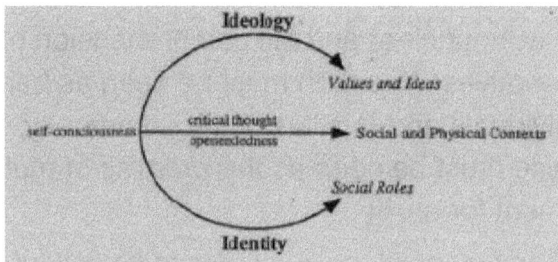

Social and physical contacts must be within the context of self-consciousness, critical thought, and open-endedness.

Normally all values and ideas (ideology) and social roles (identity) are constructed from a combination of philosophy and theology. All values and ideas plus personal and group identity are guerilla-glued to the past. Change is painfully slow and requires humility, patience and tolerance by all concerned.

Some commonalities may be substantial, and some differences may be simple expression of personal identity and heritage and are inconsequential as related to beneficial change for a larger group. If a change does not make a positive difference, it is not worth an argument. All social change must come from deep within the heart and soul and not a suggestion from outsiders. When it comes to faith-based operation, if it does not change the population of Heaven, it is not worth a discussion.

> **Sidebar:** When experienced men were needed in positions of leadership in my last pastorate, a man who had been a Leader for many years in another group refused to join the church so he could serve as a Deacon. In discussing the matter, he responded, *"I disagree with some of your theology, because of my belief in limited atonement; I believe only a limited number will get to heaven."* My response *"I also believe the number is limited to those who repent, believe and accept God's Plan. Regardless of different perspectives on atonement, only those who repent and believe will reach heaven. The way God's Plan is explained will not change the population of heaven."* The next week he and his wife joined the Church and the next term he stood for election as a Deacon. He was a good and honorable man, but our perspective on "how" the limited number would reach heaven was inconsequential. Different personal or group understanding rooted deeply in the cultural background of groups does not change God's Plan of Redemption or the population of Heaven. All must learn to live with small differences. After all we were made in the image of God, but all fingerprints and DNA are different. Groups will never be the same, just as each individual is different. Sadly, differences both attract and divide!

> **Another case in point:** A missionary started a church among the Auca Indians of Ecuador after five missionaries were killed. He was able to reach some of the Waorani people with the message of love and grace. Their culture and family traditions were not up to Evangelical standards and the pastor was instructed by stateside leaders to make drastic changes in their

lifestyle. His response, *"God saved them, He will have to make the changes. If I interfere with their family traditions early on there will be great loss."* Even when the Gospel is received it takes time for converts to be sufficiently acculturated by friends and the Holy Spirit to make drastic changes. His missionary stipend was cut off because he would not rush the situation. God give us more spiritual leaders with convictions, understanding and tolerance to leave some things in the Hands of God. The double cure that brings social and spiritual change comes slowly. Perhaps God is more tolerant than most of us. *"Where sin abounded, grace did much more abound"* Scripture is clear: when converts have not been taught, God briefly overlooks and provides time for growth in grace and knowledge. (Acts 17:30). How long did it take some of us to get our own life straighten out? Mercifully, God knows our heart!

It is difficult to be unbiased in an assessment of another's faith-based system. Those who attempt to evaluate another's faith must understand the cultural incubators which created and controlled early developed of various faith-based groups. To view the cultural and ancestral backgrounds which differentiated Catholic and Protestant development clearly demonstrates personal viewpoints which cause a variety of outcomes. Each religious group has an ethnic, national or historical origin and heritage environment which formed the nature and structure of certain aspects of their faith.

To illustrate: two men who had been taught different views on water baptism had a discussion. One had the view the Candidate must be totally immersed and the other accepted pouring or sprinkling as sufficient. During the discussion one asked: "*You mean if one is in the water and water covers all but the forehead it is an invalid baptism?* The answer was *"YES!"* The retort, *"Since the forehead seems to be the most important* *this is why I pour or sprinkle to be certain the forehead gets wet."* Yet, it is doubtful that their differences changed the population of heaven. Is there sufficient evidence in scripture to break fellowship with others who have different views of the mode of baptism or how communion is served or on forms of worship? There will be honest differences in under-standing a portion of scripture because of language, culture or ancestral heritage?

Most followers of faith-based groups are blinded by their own cultural and ancestorial background to see all the relevant factors which formulated even their own belief system much less the faith-based behavior of others. Neither do they see the process which produced the faith-based groups with which they may disagree. This suggests the use of extreme caution in critiquing another's faith-based system. Customs and traditions are almost as difficult to handle as are the elements dealing with faith. Note the response in Jerusalem to the conversion of Gentiles which brought *great rejoicing and controversy.*

5. But certain of the converted Pharisees, said, that it was necessary to circumcise converts *and to require them to keep the Law of Moses. 6. The apostles and elders came together to consider the question. 7. After a heated discussion,* <u>Peter stood up and said, Brethren, you well know that in the past God made a choice that through my words the Gentiles should hear the gospel and learn to believe. 8. And God who knows the hearts of men, gave evidence of this by bestowing on them the Holy Spirit just as He did on us; 9. And God made no distinctions between us and them by cleansing their hearts by faith.</u> *10.* **Why do you now attempt to provoke God**

and put a yoke on believers which neither our fathers nor we were able to bear? (Acts 15:5-10 EDNT)

28. For it seemed good to the Holy Spirit and to us, not to impose any extra burden on you, apart from the necessary ones: 29. that you abstain from food sacrificed to idols, from tasting blood, from things strangled, and from sexual immorality: if you guard against these things, you will be doing right. Be strong! (Acts 15:28-29 EDNT)

There must be transparency of intent in dealing with people and groups in a multicultural community. Most are suspicious of any effort to change the existing state of affairs, particularly with reference to social interaction, family life and/or faith-based worship. Culture is deeply rooted in the heart and soul and woven into the fabric of their faith-based thinking of individuals. This is expressed in the foods they prefer, the music they enjoy, the clothes they wear, the customs they practice, and the traditions handed down from previous generations which influence their worship. All change must be slow and in small increments and work within the framework of general acceptance. Any attempt to rush the process beyond the normal capacity to accept change is to stop the progress of constructive change.

A couple intending to be married come from different backgrounds and at times from different faith-based systems. During the courting period *"attraction and affection"* hides multiple differences. Later family heritage, as part of the glue which holds things together, begins to influence the outcome of discussions. Little things: such as, food preparation, housekeeping, personal habits, in-laws, worship styles, music preference and extended family become a "deal breaker" and over time things fall apart. The percentage of marriages which fail between two people who love each other is an example of how cultural background influences relationships in addition there is input from parents, in-laws, siblings, aunt Mary, Uncle John and grandpa's old pastor.

Friendship is a boat in which to sail the troubled seas of relationship which requires expert knowledge. In fact, the Greek term *cybernetics* has complicated and sophisticated meanings, but actually means *helmsman* – one who steers the boat. The question in relationships is clearly who is steering the boat, who is the navigator guiding both crew and passengers through the dangerous waters? The working formula for relationship is simple: that is, the **number of people, times the number minus one equals the quantity of interpersonal relationships.** Look at the numbers: 1 x 0 = 0; that is a couple alone is a spouse minus a spouse and that equals zero.

If a couple attempts to solve a problem within themselves, they are hopelessly divided. A marriage needs a third party known as an arbitrator or mediator with godly skills to see both sides of a disagreement and negotiate an acceptable outcome. Since Solomon is no longer around, the only true mediator between God and man is Jesus and He is in heaven. What is an inexperienced couple to do: pray together about the difficulty? It is the nature of humans to err and most are slow to forgive. This is why a silent partner reached in meditation, prayer and worship is better that all the others who are ready to offer free advice to a young couple.

The dynamics of constructive social change are similar to the difficult atmosphere of domestic differences. It is not the time for a "Now I lay me down to sleep" prayer: what is needed is a curative prayer not palliative care.

This formula *(number times number minus one) equals number of Interactive relationships* clearly demonstrates that as the number involved increases there are more perspectives applied to a discussion. This can be good or bad when attempting to solve relationship problems or make cultural changes. Unless one is "all knowing" it is best to approach a difficult community situation with prayer, transparency, objective detachment and listening with neutrality to all voices.

This is why constructive social change in a community is similar to the resolution of marriage problems. Both require objective assistance rather that subjective or biased input. Also, group problems are assigned to committees with guidance or action groups with a focused task agenda. In the days when Jesus walked the earth, He made a difference in slaves and servants who were in a cultural trap and a developed trust in relationship that matured into friendship. There is a place in the process of close association that relationship matures from servant to workmate, to colleague, to companion, to comrade and genuine friendship. As one grows and learns they began to clearly understand the nature of the environment and developed a realistic view of where they fit into the future participation. Jesus said:

> *15. I no longer call you bond-slaves; because a bond-slave does not know what his lord does: but you I have called **friends**; for all things that I*

have heard of my Father I have made known to you. 16. **You have not chosen me, but I have chosen you, and appointed you to go out and bring in fruit, and that your fruit should remain: and that you should obtain answers to your prayers to make them**

This clearly points that transparency develops friendship, trust and understanding. The first step in recruiting one for participation in a Together/Strong group working for constructive change is to build friendship. The person must understand they were "chosen" or selected because of their character and maturity from a large pool of possible participants to consider community problems. Friendship and prayer are crucial to participation and a free exchange of ideas. Friends share with friends and the desired constructive change moves forward step by step.

It appears that maturity and understanding comes with friendship as individuals become attached to each other and practice the transparency necessary to maintain both a social and spiritual connection. With this process comes wisdom and the understanding of social distance, personal space, family heritage, language variations, and differences in people. Attraction, attachment and affection comes with an awareness that people are different. They have different family heritage, different dreams and hopes for the future. Most also have a built-in criterion for accepting or rejecting others. The sad thing about this: most do not realize the subconscious criteria exist and controls their bias and interaction with others. This silent regulator of behavior comes from a deep place in the heart and soul of the individual and is the result of a teachable spirit. (James 1:19-25 EDNT)

19. Wherefore, my cherished band of believers, let everyone be swift to hear, slow to speak, slow to wrath: 19. because of the righteousness of God, my cherished band of believers, let everyone be ready listeners, slow to express our mind, slow to take offence: 20. for the anger does not bear fruit acceptable to God. 21. Wherefore put aside all moral corruption and the abundance of worthless behavior and **receive with a teachable spirit the firmly established word, which is able to make safe that spiritual part of you that determines all behavior.** *22. You must be honest with yourselves and live by the word not merely hear it. 23. But those who listens to the word, and do not behave it, are similar to a man seeing his own face in a mirror; 24. He observes his flaws, and immediately forgets the man he saw. 25. But whosoever bows down to observe the complete prescriptive usage and the unrestrained opportunity to continue in the word and not become a forgetful hearer, but one who behaves the prescribed deeds, this man shall by the blood be set apart for consecrated action.*

8. Finally, you must think the same thoughts, share difficulties with one another, having automatic interdependence with brotherly kindness; be tender-hearted and humble-minded: 9. you must not repay injury with injury, or hard words with hard words, but bless those who curse you. ***For you were called to give kind words to others and come to a well-spoken eulogy at the end.*** *10. For the one wishing to love life and see prosperous days, let him avoid an evil tongue and cunning words. 11. Habitually avoid evil and do* *good; let him seek and follow peace. 12. Because the eyes of the Lord watch over the righteous, and his ears listen to their payers: but the Lord looks directly into the eyes of wrongdoers.* (1 Peter 3:8-12 EDNT)

Those who belong to different faith-based and cultural groups must clearly see how they are viewed by others before they condemn another's faith or evaluate their lifestyle or ancestorial backgrounds. Any effort to cause a personal break with ancestorial traditions and culture will solicit a negative response and prompt an argument. Coming to a conclusion that personal attitudes and behavior must be changed will create a disconnect with ancestorial background and cause pain and suffering in family groups. Many see change in traditional behavior as a personal rejection of family heritage. This requires patience and wisdom: first patience to search for common ground; then the wisdom of Solomon to minimize differences. Sacred writings are clear:

5. If any of you lack wise judgment, let him express the craving by words to God, that gives to all men liberally, and does not defame, chide or snatch away your joy, and it shall be given him. 6. But let him ask in faith, nothing wavering, for he that shows doubt or indecision is like a wave of the sea driven with the wind and tossed. (James 1:5,6 EDNT)

GOD'S GIFT OF CHILDREN

Children need guidance from caring adults.
They must feel safe and secure in a sheltered place.
No one can fully replace a Mother's love and care.
Yet, stand-in caregivers are a God-sent blessing!

Children need biological parents in the home.
Otherwise; watch care is required by surrogates.
Both girls and boys crave two parents plus a village
To assist them climbing life's Hill of Difficulty.

Children want connectedness with loving adults to
Bond and develop a positive personality and a
Knowledge base of subject matter and experience to
Become a moral citizen in the public square.

Children must be educated for the marketplace.
And guided by loving adults to find a mate.
An extended family must demonstrate a stability
And resourcefulness as an example of citizenship.

Children are gifts from a Heavenly Father entrusted
To adults to prepare them for living and the Afterlife.
And taught to value friends and the worth-ship of
An ever-present, benevolent and personal God.

—H. Lynn Green (2020)

Chapter Four

ASSIMILATE
SOLOMON'S WISDOM

*Social change is not cooperation to construct
a least common faith-based denominator or
that ethnic groups should lose their culture or
compromise their sacred reality. Culture and
tradition are the social glue which holds people
together. Groups have a right to maintain their
cultural identity. Yet, compromise, a (together-
promise) contract, is required to affirm an
agreement. This is the starting point for social
and/or spiritual change, and requires the
Wisdom of Solomon.*

These are troubled and dangerous times for the
dominant culture and the present way of life in many
parts of the world. There is great need for wisdom and
courage to assist moral and ethical people as they
navigate the cultural confusion to affirm common ground
and minimize differences. Yes, we are warned not to
trust the wisdom of men or follow those with cleaver
words; however, each time in history when constructive
change was required mature leaders were able to
formulate a workable plan. Often the principal leader was

one who had been chosen and prepared by family for a productive life. At times this person was weak but willing to seek divine assistance to generate the strength to lead people step by step in the right direction.

Do we need another Abraham, a new Moses, a Joshua or Caleb? Perhaps we need only a shepherd boy who trusts God and a sling and 5 stones to fight the giants! Could we find a Washington, a Roosevelt or a Churchill? Perhaps there is a respected man of the cloth who is totally submissive to the will of God. Certainly, we need individuals with the commitment of Naomi and Ruth who created a stable future for themselves and their family.

> *"Intreat me not to leave you, or to return from following you: for where you go, I will go; and where you live, I will live; your people shall be my people and your God will be my God."*

Solomon's father provided guidance on how to function as a King, but Solomon remained inadequate for the task and prayed for wisdom. He demonstrated insight and good judgement. Yet, Solomon saw value in asking others to participate in the process of finding workable solutions. He understood that he alone could not do everything and needed to add others to effectively deal with the diversity of existing problems.

Chosen leaders must be respected: otherwise, there is civil disobedience, mutiny and rampage. The ancient record is clear: without trusted leaders, informed individuals must seek out mature individuals with experience and secure their counsel on significant matters. Often a "Together/Strong" NETWORK was formed of those willing to seek guidance and assistance from a Higher Power.

Solomon asked God for wisdom. God honored his request, and he became known as a wise leader. All who seek to lead others during difficult times, must be wise; that is, informed on the issues at hand, clever and shrewd in the decision process, and practical and sensible in presenting possible solutions.

> *3. Those with good conduct have nothing to fear because established authorities are against the wrongdoer. Do you want to have no fear of authorities? Then do what is good, and you will receive praise: 4. for the magistrate is the minister of God to you for good. But if you do wrong, you have reason to be alarmed; for the sword of justice is not without meaning, for the magistrates are the ministers of God to execute punishment to the evil doer. 5.* **Therefore you must line up under authority, not only to escape God's anger, but also because it is the right thing to do***.*
> (Romans 13:3-5 EDNT)

The established order is for the good of all; destroy it and all suffer loss. Good people and good families must stand together and resist behavior that is deficient of common sense and social order. The collective good must work together to limit evil influence on society and all malicious and unlawful behavior must be restricted to orderly protest. Any activity which promotes and sustains disruptive behavior will weaken central authority and endanger liberty and justice for all. Dissent and opposition must be limited to peaceful protest organized and supervised by respected and trusted leadership.

All disagreements may be unscrambled by honest negotiation which leads to compromise and reconciliation. The term *"compromise"* is not a bad word it simply means *"together with promise."* This is the essence of a *"contract"* in which both sides come together and give up or change something to get something better. Normally, this process requires a third party as an arbitrator (peacemaker) for both sides to win! This cannot be accomplished in the streets but requires a controlled environment and at least two participants together with an arbitrator to reach an acceptable outcome.

An arbitrator must possess the wisdom of Solomon in understanding the problem and be able to arrange and lead the participants in a positive process for an acceptable outcome. Solomon's recorded decisions exhibited knowledge, honest perception and good judgment by avoiding unilateral action. By including other voices, he multiplied his effort to solve problems. He wisely permitted others the right to speak their feelings which enabled a reasonable decision in a truth-based solution in a life and death situation. The general principle is that there is wisdom in seeking a wide range of advice. (Proverbs 15:22). We could learn by assimilating the wisdom of Solomon. In Ecclesiastes 4:9-12 he wrote:

> [9] **Two are better than one,** *because they have a good reward for their labor.* [10] *For if they fall, the one will lift up his fellow: but woe to him that is alone when he falls; for he hath not another to help him up.* [11] *Again, if two lies together, then they have heat: but how can one be warm alone?* [12] *And if one prevails against him, two shall withstand him; and* **a threefold cord is not quickly broken.**

Solomon's problem-solving process demonstrated doable ways humans could work together to accomplish common good and facilitate positive outcomes. One working alone may achieve something but the value of multiplication can cause others to join in the process and improve the outcome. When others add to the solution, they feel their contribution was an essential part of the outcome. More is accomplished and all have a good reward for their labor. This could be applied together with physical labor for additional reward. Then Solomon introduced the warmness of the marriage bed on a wintry night. He also recognized the discomfort of sleeping alone on a cold night. Most importantly, Solomon recognized that a threefold cord was not easily broken.

Solomon's wisdom used common sense with practical first-hand knowledge. Provided this is applied to wedlock where a man *"pursues a bride until she catches him"* and intimacy follows wedlock and ultimately a child is born. Solomon declared the outcome to be a *"threefold cord is not quickly broken."* Perhaps this is the bonding which comes with the first child when the gene pool of two families are joined to produce an offspring and the weaving of a threefold unity becomes a reality and the family unit is strengthened, and a family legacy is assured, and the world becomes a better place.

Change advocates should take a cue from Solomon about the increase of strength by adding another interested party such as a spouse and how the addition of the threefold cord creates a family bond. Could this be applied to the process of constructive change in a multicultural group? This writer affirms the data is relevant to the multicultural state of many communities.

The end is worth the journey, but facts suggest that positive social change is a long and incremental process.

Just how does one go about producing positive social change in the midst of multiple and mixed cultures, different languages, various traditions and conflicting religions? How does one construct a process which leads to a cooperative effort for constructive change? This can never be a one-man show or the work of a few, a team is best.

> **Sidebar:** A story from Grandfather Green during my childhood taught me the value of getting others involved in problem solving. It seems that a man had several sons and one day he lined them all up and gave each one a small stick. Then, he asked each one to break his stick. It was an easy task. Discarding the broken sticks, the father gave each one another stick and asked them to combine their sticks with the one next to them and break them. It was harder but still the sticks were broken. The process continued until the bundle of sticks could not be broken by the strongest son. What was the lesson? The brothers learned that some problems could be solved by just one and with others more assistance was needed because the task was greater. Finally, they came to realize there were areas of concern that all of them together could not solve and would have to seek additional strength from others.... Then the father presented the final lesson! **Some problems could only be solved with divine assistance**.

This is how to navigate a way forward in a multi-cultural environment. Each group must be represented, and each person must do their best depending on the assistance of God and others. Some problems can only be solved through a strong committed group which includes prayer and fasting plus the touch of the Hand of God. Such is similar to the growing of a garden which requires several steps in the process. An uncultivated field must be turned into a productive garden to provide food for the family table. Constructive social change in a multicultural community is similar to the steps in growing a family garden.

Diligent cultivation is the first step in growing a garden. It is painstaking and persistent work on fallow ground before a seed is planted. When the groundwork is prepared, there must be careful and prayerful planting of seeds which hopefully will grow into a useful crop. After planting unceasing effort is required to keep weeds from hindering growth. Constant attention must be shown to all aspects of the garden: does it have sufficient nutrition, enough water, adequate weeding, and some resowing for the seed which did not mature. Then comes saintly patience with the process of growth; it cannot be hurried. Overzealous attention can cause the law of diminishing returns to operate that actually hinders the size and delays the harvest. In spite of the hard work and the "green thumb" knowledge of the workers, growing a garden is a partnership with God. The garden must be touched by the finger of God to produce a good harvest.

Those who wish to initiate social and/or spiritual change in a multicultural community must follow the injunction *"seek first the kingdom of God and other things will be added,"* but prayer and meditative planning alone is not sufficient for spiritual change in a community. An atmosphere conducive to constructive change must exist before individuals are willing to consider social change. Normally, most people need a spiritual nudge to move toward personal and positive change. Scripture is clear: The spiritual is not first, but the natural: and afterward the spiritual. (1 Corinthians 15:46) Individuals must be assisted with initial change in behavior before they see the need for moral, ethical and spiritual change.

A structured framework for social change is a precursor to spiritual change. Once individuals see the benefit of social change, they become open to personal change. Becoming a moral citizen of society is a giant step toward becoming a mystical citizen of heaven. In spiritual conversion, the Spirit works first on the potential convert, then a human messenger shares the story of grace and forgiveness. This leads to a change of heart which prompts changed behavior and a spiritual lifestyle. Yes, there are "first things" which includes God's will and the Spirit's influence before any constructive change begins. However, there is lots of human effort prior to constructive change. Some older folk remember the hard times when families were urged to plant vegetable gardens to supplement their food supply. Growing a garden also taught families, especially the children, that God was involved in the process, but there was plenty of work for the Gardener.

Whether it is growing corn, attempting community change or reaching for faith-based understanding, curative prayer not palliative care is a good place to start. Sincere prayer by one, with two or three in agreement or the concert prayer of a group, is an essential step in problem solving in a human population. *"To err is human; to forgive is divine!"* Social change is needed because of human weakness and solved by the strength of personal prayer. Yes, individuals and groups need palliative care, but the first effort should be curative prayer. Prayer will also assist unity of the team and open the minds and hearts to the needs of the people and to the power of divine intervention. The prayer group may have to march around the walls several times before an entrance is found. Intercessory prayer works. In the words of a young girl "***Prayer is just like jam; you can't spread even a little without getting some on yourself.***

Morality is a state of being decent, honest, and principled in attitude and action. Conditions which dominate a community in the absence of high moral standards include disrespect for people, property, personal rights, murder, kidnapping, human trafficking and promiscuous sexual behavior.

Chapter Five

ACCEPT

COMMON MORAL BENCHMARKS

The use of the construct "moral standards" describes something that could be benchmarked and used as a reference point for comparative evaluation. All groups have moral values and expected behavior of all involved. Family units have moral expectations of each other. Organizations and institutions have rules of conduct for their members. Professions have ethical standards. Faith-based groups normally base their expectations of morality on sacred writings while secular society uses common sense and experience to make rules to follow in relationships and all human interaction. This does not mean that such rules are always followed or that outdated rules are appropriately relevant for the present environment. Regretfully, many expect better conduct and deportment from others than they practice themselves. The lack of compliance to moral standards makes matters worse.

Never neglect the wisdom of mothers in structuring moral standards. Mothers seem to have insight to behavior that could cause problems later. Before there were benevolent governments or institutions of higher learning, mothers prepared their children as moral leaders. Children are the legacy of families and mothers are the gatekeepers of morality. Fathers also assist in this effort, but in comparison mothers are the *"better half"* of the partnership in raising children to be moral citizens of the community. If you need to develop the criteria for a moral standard, always listen to those experienced in the nurturing of children.

Criteria built into ethical and moral standards are based on personal acts and human interaction believed to be acceptable and decent. Simply, attitudes and behaviors which benefit society are judged to be moral. Those matters which seriously harm individuals and social order are judged to be morally wrong. Different groups may have their own benchmarks for moral and acceptable deportment. This may include attitude, attire as well as action. Most professions have ethical standards to guide members behavior and deal harshly with those who violate the expected norms. When the dominant culture or primary governance is weakened the standard of moral behavior deteriorates.

When a community has a high score on the morality scale which includes correctness, decency, honesty and integrity, people are confident, respectful and productive. Normally, families function lovingly and peacefully; the community is happy, safe, united in its diversity, with a positive view of the future. Adhering to a plan to uphold a recognized level of decency and respect defines a constructive method to reach a desired social order. Strategy is the art and science of planning and marshalling resources for their most efficient and effective use. Humans are normally relational. Good relationships on all levels contribute to the health and productivity of individuals, groups and communities.

A workable strategy is to identify individuals and relationships that are hindered by immoral activity and determine the beneficial lessons to be taught to the next generation.   This ensures the maintenance of the moral high ground in a given population.

Provided one can become a change agent rather than only a catalyst in an effort to establish the moral high ground, the change must start with those who suggest change. A catalyst may be an agent of change but does not change in the process. To influence moral excellence in the family, community and place of worship, change must start with the individuals in charge. In sacred writings when asked about which commandment was in first position, the answer was clear: personal behavior influences the attitude and actions of others.

> *30. And thou shall love the Lord your God with your whole heart, and with your whole existence, and with all your moral understanding, and with all your ability and strength: 31.* **namely this, you shall love as yourself those near you. There is no other commandment greater than these***.* (Mark 12:28-31 EDNT)

The beneficial features of this relationship are character, identity, self-esteem, values, skills, and attitude. Goal setting, training, and evaluations will be used in self-development. Areas of the self-improvement must focus on the physical, mental, social, emotional, and spiritual.

A priority relationship begins within the family and is vital to the individual, community, and society. The breakdown of the family is a repairable problem, but few seem to care even those most affected. Statistics reveal that one out of every two marriages ultimately fail but unknown is the number of couples who endure a flawed relationship for the false positive benefit of the children. Paul writing about a problem marriage was clear that domestic problems produce "*defiled children*" (1 Corinthians 7:14). Daily the news reports children being sexually molested, abandoned, and even killed by family members. Some of the major areas of concern are charity, responsibility, authority, accountability, sexuality, integrity, and spirituality. These issues can be dealt with through family meetings, training, seminars, recreation, and the establishing and maintaining of behavioral boundaries.

Children are molested by more than family: trusted youth organizations, orphanages, boarding schools, and the bad example of political leaders and sports heroes. However, the most tragic is the trusted religious groups which condone or cover up the immorality of leaders under their supervision. If we can no longer trust leaders of youth organizations or pedophiles who masquerade as leaders of religious organizations, whom shall we trust?

This writer believes there is a "*bottomless pit*" prepared for the devil and those who blaspheme God by pretending to be a faithful servant and all the while condoning or molesting the innocent.

42. And whoever shall cause to stumble or entice to sin* one of these little ones who believes in Me, it is better for him that a large grinder-stone be wrapped around his neck and be thrown into the sea. (Mark 9:42 EDNT)

*v42 "offend" is skandalizo the English "scandalize"
and means to "stumble, entrap, trip up or entice to sin."
Obviously, Jesus saw the abuse of children as a serious
matter. It appears that receiving children brings personal
responsibility.

The individuals who join themselves to a local
assembly for worship must manifest the character
exhibited in the fruit of the Spirit, obey the commands
of scripture, and fulfil the Challenge of Jesus to *"make
disciples as they go into all the world,"* initiating and
teaching converts all that Jesus taught and follow pure
religion standards and keep themselves *"untainted
with immorality."* The establishing of small cohorts for
fellowship and prayer in the various enclaves of the
community with the goal of being holistic in their service
to God and man will contribute significantly to the
moral well-being of the people. Lessening the mistrust
and cooperating with other faith-based groups in the
community will also contribute to the restoration of the
moral high ground.

The faith-based diversity, business complexity, ethnic
plurality, social complexity, political issues, and economic
problems, all contribute to the mistrust. A strategy that
will restore and maintain morality in the community would
require individuals and groups to lessen mistrust, protect
the rights of one another, participate in cultural activities,
and provide programs for individuals and groups that will
address the fundamental issues of the community.

Attention must be given to relationships in the
workplace. Employment issues revolve around the
employer and the employee. Some of the major issues
are wages, health, safety, authority and responsibility,

interpersonal relationship, human resource, unions, insurance, skills training, rights, evaluation, promotion, discrimination and harassment. An employment strategy must include the welfare of the employer and the employee. The employer should adopt a positive attitude towards all employees which creates an environment conducive to employee participation. Employee behavior should come from a fair and respectful attitude and a sense of personal responsibility to the business and its leaders.

Without positive attitudes of all parties, constructive social change will be difficult in the whole community. Problems at work usually spill over at home and other group gatherings.

One unpopular note: Satan as a Roaring Lion goes about seeking whom to devour. The major issues in this relationship are temptations, harassments, strongholds, and control. The strategy would involve personal resistance to temptations, cohort resistance of strong-holds, and gifted leaders providing guidance toward positive change. Corruption undermines good governance and produces negative consequences for all citizens. Government was established to serve the people by advancing harmony and preventing chaos.

A positive governance strategy would consider the welfare of all citizens and would provide feedback for the disadvantaged. It would provide a mechanism for the development, direction, and equitable distribution of human and material resources. Finally, there must be no infringement on the rights of free and open worship of a Higher Power. The ways and means various groups approach and maintain their spiritual devotion abolished or condemned. Any change in spiritual behavior must generate from withing the heart and soul of individuals and not dictated by secular powers or sectarian leadership. The basic issue is how, when and when individual demonstrate their devotion to their stated deity.

All individuals or groups who wish to facilitate constructive change in a community must seriously take into account both the culture and the faith-based foundational heritage of all groups. All interested in changing others must understand had you been born in their culture into their family and were taught about faith in their system, *"There but for the grace of God are you!" We all learn from teachers in a single environment and according to Jesus "the learner is not above his teacher..."* and does not reach beyond the teacher's level (unless there is additional social and spiritual guidance.

> *39. And Jesus used a story, saying: Surely the blind cannot guide the blind or both will fall into a ditch? 40.* **The learner is not above his teacher: but everyone who is fully taught will reach his teacher's level.** *41. And why do you see the speck in your brother's eye but cannot recognize the beam in your own eye? 42.* **How can you say to your brother Let me get the speck out of your eye, when you observe not the beam in your own eye?** *You insincere talker, begin by removing the beam from your own eye, and then you may see clearly to remove the speck in your brother's eye. (Luke 6:39-42 EDNT)*

Words and symbols have both positive
and negative influence on people
because of their deep roots in culture.
When words are not understood,
recognizable symbols are used to
create meaning without words.
Symbols also create a nonverbal
message and establish an atmosphere
from a cultural perspective. Symbols
have an indelible impression and will
not be changed easily.

Chapter Six

AVOID
CULTURAL AND SYMBOLIC BARRIERS

Symbols are used to express ideas and values to constituency by most groups and institutions. My family migrated from England many years ago, but the culture of old England remains deeply engrained in the Green family. My English Family Crest is on proud display in my home. Many English guests have graced my home and my many trips to the University of Oxford for research at the Bodleian Library has been an active part of academic life. The meaning of words and symbols were conceptualized in the language and culture where they developed. Difficulty exists when these concepts are used in a different environment.

Sidebar: Geoffrey Thomas, PhD with the University of Oxford, came to Tennessee to speak at Degree Day and shared that England and America were separated by a common language. He further illustrated by describing names the UK uses for parts of an automobile: *gasoline is petrol, hood is the bonnet, windshield is windscreen, the fenders were mudguards, the bumpers were overriders, the trunk was the boot, etc.* Then he explained some words had different meanings, for example, *momentarily* in the US means **in a moment**; in the UK m*omentarily* means

for a moment. Dr. Thomas shared his leaving London airport, when the pilot announced, "*We will be taking off **momentarily** so buckle your seat belts.*" What he understood was, *"We will be leaving the ground **for a moment** and come right back down!"* **Yes, he cinched his safety belt snug tight.**

Similar misunderstanding occurs when certain words or technical terms are used in places of worship. Words and symbols are interpreted differently according to one's culture because they create an atmosphere that may be recognized as an icon which may become an idol for adoration and reverence. This takes away from the genuine worship which is a true feeling of the worth and value of God in all aspects of life.

Faith-based living in the purest form is free from blemish and clean without contamination by human intrusion into the sacred. In scripture, pure religion was free from extraneous matter; it simply expressed concern for morality and the needs of the fatherless and women lacking a husband's watch care. There was no need for elaborate buildings, ornate furniture or manmade symbols. Nothing was to distract from the simplicity of the worship and witness. A precise picture of this pure and pristine faith is clear in the Book of James, which many believe is the oldest preserved New Testament writing.

> *7. Free from all that would dim the transparency in belief and conduct before God and the Father is this, to go see and relieve the orphans without a father's protection and the women lacking a husband in their distress, and to keep himself untainted with guilt. (James 1:27 EDNT)*

During the first 100 years after the Upper Room experience, the early travelers on the straight and narrow "way," were devoted to worship in various sacred places including the central sanctuary of the temple and in houses of believers. In fact, the Greek phrase "house-to-house" were homes of believers that were turned into "*extension sanctuaries*" for worship, shelter and safety. Early believers were at first all Jewish converts, then Greek speaking Jews, then Gentile converts.

> *1. Those who willingly received his word, were baptized: and the same day about three thousand souls were added to the believers. 42. And they continued consistently in the apostles' doctrine and fellowship, and in breaking of bread, and in prayers. 43. Everyone was filled with a sense of reverence: and many signs and wonders were done by the apostles. 44. All who believed kept together, and all their possessions were shared; 45. Goods and property were sold and distributed as every man had need. 46. And they agreed to meet daily in the temple and to break bread from house to house, and they took meals cheerfully and with personal commitment. 47. Praising God and having favor with all the people. And the Lord added to the congregation daily those being saved. (Acts 2:46-47 EDNT)*

During the first century, local groups grew sufficiently that local homes could not accommodate the numbers. The homes as gathering places became too small and special purpose buildings were built. Sadly, the buildings became filled with ornate icons: paintings, images, idols, and symbols to represent words to communicate to those who did not read. Then they became sacred and became idols for worship. Part of the value of the Reformation was the abandonment of the accumulation of these icons and their representation became so convoluted that mixed messages were sent to the people. An occurrence during the Reformation was the aggressive removal of pictures, images, stained glass, candles, fonts and other traditional icons from places of worship. After the Reformation, the less a building looked like a Cathedral the more it was used for worship, while the ornate structures became museums to exhibit art and Artifex and visit occasionally on special days.

As special purpose buildings grew beyond places of worship and took on a museum-type quality and became more of an exhibit hall or icon center, the places of worship gradually became less of a holy place for true worship where the faithful gathered to show the worth and value of God in their lives. This is in contrast to an occasionally visited museum to see a relic of the past, historic artifact, or a Saint's image in a stained-glass window. Tragically the condition continues. When buildings failed to resemble places of worship from the past, the more they were used for worship alone. Later they came up with a rationale for the use of colored glass to make pictures for the windows and gradually added back symbols and images. As the buildings changed, so the people and their worship changed. This also altered the way the community viewed the buildings and their perception of those who attended. This is also true of children and grandchildren who are influenced by the previous generation. Grand-parents and parents still have powerful influence on children, both good and bad.

The craft of stained-glass art is a complicated process using spooled lead and cut pieces of colored glass to form pictorial designs and religious icons. The designs are of people and specialized symbols. At times the symbols are misunderstood; for example, Anglicans and Catholics us a Crucifix, to represent Jesus on the Cross, while Protestants use an empty cross to express the Resurrection. This viewing of the Cross through the Empty Tomb signifies a much different message. Many symbols have a kind of double entendre and an unintended ambiguity comes from words or symbols with more than one interpretation. Also, when words are translated, and symbols transferred from one time period and cultural to another the meaning changes. For example, the symbol of a "fish" meant one thing to early Christians and something entirely different to a Roman soldier. Today, math uses a fishlike symbol (a stretched-out *alpha* which resembles a fish and means "proportion to.")

Symbols are not all bad, but they mean more to the young because they are normally ignored by adults. Perhaps the key to pure religion is to become a "saint," but what is a saint? A young boy was asked this question and his answer was surprising, *"A Saint is someone the light shines through."* Asked for additional information as to how he came up with that answer, *"I learned about saints in the morning worship service. You see the stained-glass windows had pictures of Saints and the sunlight would shine through the pictures...a saint is someone the light shines through!"* What he knew about saints was from sunlight and stained-glass windows. It was a good definition of a saint and a profound grasp of letting God's light shine through you. And perhaps gave some meaning to a stained-glass window in a sanctuary.

Sidebar: in Lima, Peru the week the Pope defrocked several saints whom he believed had been elevated improperly. There to write a story and searched for someone who could speak English better that I could Spanish. A young man about 25 was willing to talk with me. He was asked his opinion about the Pope's action. His answer, "The Pope was correct but said we could still pray to them if it were habitual and we were not to teach the children to pray to them." Another question, "Why do you pray to saints?" His response was firm and enlightening, "Saints do not answer our prayers, God does. Saints are only reminders to pray for specific things and at certain times." I asked, "What is a saint?" *...a Saint is someone who lives so good that when they die, they do not have to go to Purgatory, they go straight to Heaven.*" By his definition, I was a Saint and would go straight to Heaven.

Reaching my hand to shake his, *"I am Saint Hollis."* He turned pale and backed away swiftly, then turned and ran half a block to a church and looked back. He thought I was one of those defrocked saints that had appeared to him. The next time my travels take me to Lima, I will go to that corner to see if there is a statue to "Saint Hollis." Stranger things have happened.

Does God's light shine through you? The stained-glass barrier could easily be broken if worshipers understood that they must go out into the community and let God's light shine through them. It would be good to remember that John, The Baptist was a "burning and shining light." Tragically, many so called believers' lifestyle does not reflect the light of God in their behavior because of moral darkness. Such a negative witness will never convince others of the true light of God reflected through moral behavior. Lifestyle influences social change.

33. No man who lights a lamp puts it in a closet, nor under a box, but on a lamp stand so all may see the light. 34. The lamp of the body is the eye: therefore, when your eye is focused your whole body has light; but when your eye is morally bad, your body is full of darkness. 35. **Take care that the reflected light in you does not come from moral darkness.** *36. If you have light for the body with the absence of darkness, the whole shall be light, as when a candle shines brightly in the dark. (Luke 11:33-36 EDNT)*

Sacred writings furnish ample precedent for a personal and persistent involvement in the marketplace rather that an occasional activity in the stained -glass ghetto island used as a place of worship. The true expression of God grace is often viewed through cultural glasses and the interpretation of truth differs from group to group. The wearing of cultural clothes associated with a particular brand of faith also confuses the public. The obvious question, "Why does God dress His people so differently?" This has produced a half-filled sanctuary cloistered behind stained glass windows with half-hearted commitment to the basic tenets of faith. A well-rehearse choir sings beautifully, but the community is not there to hear. The pulpit has a "talking head" to whom no one listens, but lapsed time is duly noted. There must be a person-to-person witness outside the sanctuary to break the stained-glass barrier that hinders many from receiving the message of love and grace.

A visit to Jamaica early in my ministry, was eventful. My host showed me around the island and explained local customs. We attended religious services, visited politicians, saw a few Rastafarians with dreadlocks, heard some peculiar music, and bought a few things at the straw market. Jamaica is a place of beauty and full of history, tradition, and different cultures.

A native girl working in the missionary's home served meals, watched after the children and cleaned the house. One morning she was not present to serve breakfast. The next morning, she returned and being inadequately informed in their culture my words, "You were missed yesterday" were not suitable. This was obviously not an appropriate comment from an American to make to a young Jamaican girl. She self-consciously explained she had gone to visit her mother, but this Southern boy responded that she had gone to visit a boyfriend. She was shocked and hurt by this assumption and snapped back, *"I am a Christian! I do not have a boyfriend!"*

After the young lady left the room, my host explained that she had been insulted. At that period in Jamaican history, moral young people did not date or meet with the opposite sex without parental permission and supervision. My false assumption had accused her of being sexually active. After this experience, my words were selected more carefully when dealing with people in other cultures. It was a lesson learned: well-intended words and actions mean different things in various cultures. While speaking in Japan and trying to say something nice about the pastor's wife, in my broken Japanese she was called *"a cute chicken."* Finally, my hard lesson was learned.

Growing up in Chattanooga, Tennessee, the problem of race was never a consideration. There were segregated schools and buses, but it was natural for that period of southern history. It was just accepted, but my paternal Grandfather taught me not to discriminate against people on the basis of color, but to use character, personality, and faith as criteria for acceptance. He would use his hand to show what he meant. *"Just as the open hand, people are separated on many social issues, but as the closed fist, people are together in times of trouble."* This was good guidance for a growing boy before the Civil Rights movement came along.

As a teenager, my family lived on the edge of the Black community and the children associated freely with children their own age. It was hard to understand why we could not attend the same school, but mother explained that the City Fathers drew district lines, and the line ran down the middle of our street. Sharing with mother my dislike of their line, *"They should keep their cotton-picking hands out of our business."* The children had developed good community relationships; it was the older folk with a negative agenda that the children did not understand. Prejudice views are taught, children are not born with such ideas. Prejudice comes from adults usually out of selfishness or stupidity.

During high school, my weekend job was at a grocery store across the city. Walking home one Friday without bus fare, it was a long walk of several miles, but my friend, Willie Wise, drove by and picked me up. *"Why are you walking man, this is a bad part of town!"* Realizing my preference would be to ride, he gave me a ride, let me out near my home, then handed me bus fare to get to work the next morning. A kind gesture confirmed Willie as a friend. He was older and had been in the army. Life had not been easy for him; Willie was black, but he recognized the need of a poor friend. Willie was what my Grandfather called a "giver." The world would be a better place if there were more wise men like Willie Wise! Color did not matter, it was character, consideration, and courage that counted.

My experience with Willie Wise made me more conscious of the problem of race. At every opportunity, my feelings are expressed about segregation. Being from the south and studying at the University of Cincinnati, a sociology professor put me on the debate team against segregation. We won the debate with the argument that discrimination against people of color only happened when they sat down. They could stand in line, order food, buy stuff, even stand on the bus up front, but if they sat down everybody else stood in protest. My solution was to put stand up desks in the schools, take all the seats out of public buses and make everyone stand, take the benches out of public parks and places of worship (at that period even the churches were segregated), using an idea from history that the rulers had a throne or a seat of authority as the symbol of power, such as, a seat on the Supreme Court. Jews stood up to read the Torah in the Temple to illustrate that the authority was in the Word not in the reader.

Somehow, the Ohio college audience was convinced that bigotry and prejudice were based on an attempt to keep people of color out of positions of authority and that it was more political and cultural than it was racial. My efforts were noticed by Dr. Martin Luther King, Jr. and just before Dr. King died, he composed a list of 100 men most interested in Civil Rights in the South. My name appeared on that list. It has been a source of pride through the years.

My consideration for the Equal Opportunity position at the Pentagon by both Carter and Reagan was based on my Civil Rights work. The actual position was Deputy Assistant Secretary of Defense for Equal Opportunity and was responsible for protecting minorities both military and civilian in relation to the Armed Forces. At that time, about 18 million people were under the Equal Opportunity provisions of the Pentagon. Maj. Gen. Jerry R. Curry, USA, was my primary sponsor, but Senator Bill Brock (Rep.TN) cleared me politically with the White House. With these things in order, Mr. Nafziger, interviewed me at the Pentagon, showed me an office and introduced several high-ranking military officers who worked in the E. O. Division.

Mr. Nofzinger, as President Reagan's representative, asked me a straight question, *"Dr. Green, being a member of the cloth, could you enforce the Equal Opportunity provisions on 18 million people?"* My answer was direct and honest, *"For many years, my effort has been to encouraged people to associate freely along the concepts of equal opportunity. Honestly, my feeling of reluctancy about using authority to force people to comply does not fit my character or my disposition."* President Carter had offered me the same position and with this bit of self-disclosure, interest in the position again vanished and Mr. Nofzinger was asked to thank Mr. Reagan, but my withdrawal was firm. He asked, *"What will you do?* My answer was firm, "*move to Tennessee and start a new graduate school."*

My White Paper affirming that *"Only the Majority can Protect the Minority"* was sent to President Reagan. The paper explained that when a woman had the Pentagon position, she assisted blacks and Hispanics, but was unable to do much for women. The same was true when a Black or Hispanic held the position. They assisted others but were unable to facilitate the advancement of their own minority. The paper called for the elimination of all lower E. O. positions in the Pentagon and asked that the authority and accountability for Equal Opportunity remain at the highest offices where power and resources were available to actually do something. The lower E. O. offices could only agitate and litigate and probably cause more frustration than good.

Surprisingly, my ideas were worthy, and many positions were abolished. Equal Rights made good progress when those in authority were held accountable rather that passing the buck to some underling where little was ever accomplished. My move to Tennessee laid the foundation stones of Oxford Graduate School/ACRSS (American Centre for Religion/Society Studies), and pioneered the sociological integration of religion and society supported by social scientific research. (www.ogs.edu).

Chapter Seven

ADVANCE

CONSTRUCTIVE COMMUNITY CHANGE

There is sameness in a human population regardless of location or constituency. Similar problems or difficulties exist, and solving these through social change has common elements of expression and similar variables. Therefore, the process of change is structured and the transfer of this knowledge may be useful in community change.

Do you have a personal stake in a constructive outcome for positive change? Are you fully transparent concerning your interest in the process? Do you under-stand the complexity of the community and the positive and negative aspects of a multicultural environment? If your group achieves the objectives of beneficial change, what percentage of the community will benefit by the modification proposed? Will you be able to assemble an adequate collection of community Action Group members to secure sufficient information from the people to proceed in a positive manner? Do you know the leaders (official and unofficial) in the community? Have you identified the proponents and opponents of change?

Understanding the process of constructive change has many common elements which are useful in solving community problems through understanding the process. All truth is knowledge when understood and the academic and social research in change theory is relevant to community or institutional change. It is suggested that one look at the algebraic process of taking things apart to know and putting them back together to understand. This writer classifies this process as the algebra of sociological change.

The understanding of sociological change may be assisted by the algebraic process. Algebra is based on the concept of unknown values called variables and the value of each variable must remain the same in each problem. The sameness of social change regardless of the problem, process, or population uses the same concept of an equation, i.e., on both sides of the = sign there is equivalence or sameness and equality. The process of constructive change is the same whether it is a community, a faith-based group, an institution or a people group.

> **Sidebar:** symbols are used to relate the variables and constants,
>
> V   **Variables**
> C   **Constants**
> x   **Multiply**
> ÷   **Divide**
> +   **Add or Positive**
> —   **Subtract or Negative**
> ( ) **(Calculate inside paratheses first)**
> E   **Expressions**
>
> **e.g., (n x n − 1) = ER** [calculate the grouped symbols to define the Expression of Relationships]

Multiculturalism is a philosophical theory and a sociology construct that minority groups within a society should maintain cultural difference but share overall political and economic power. This social concept proports that reality is made up of many kinds of people. It is related to the *social or educational speculation that diversity is required for a modern society*. Remember, this is a theory not a confirmed law.

All the academic data relative to social change is relevant to constructive community change in multicultural areas. The construct of multiculturalism is an ideology that promotes the institutionalization of communities containing multiple cultures. It is generally applied to the demographic make-up of the post-WWII communities which include several cultures. The concepts are easily applied to the multicultural communities with ancestral heritage, language differences, cultural variations and religion based on country of origin, specific language or freeze-framed, faith-based teachings. Language and religion are the two most difficult and entrenched aspects of culture. Food, music, dress, and family life are other aspects of community culture that resist change, but to a lesser degree. Consequently, all community change must be carefully and comprehensively acceptable with the various groups of the community. There must be complete openness with the community residents. In fact, the change agents must work with various individuals until a particular change becomes "their idea." Suggestions from the people work better than recommendations from outsiders.

All social relationships and interactions may be divided according to (A. Fisk, 1992). Communal sharing **(CS);** authority ranking **(AR),** equality marching **(EM)** and market pricing **(MP).** Fisk claimed that all interactions may be placed in these categories. **(CS)** brings with it a sense of equivalence and follows common practices while minimizing differences. **(AR)** recognizes high ranking individuals who are respected and take responsibility where needed. **(EM)** individuals balance differences between others and themselves and share by taking turns, equally dividing tasks, to reach an even balance. **(MP)** residents maintain socially significant consideration in prices, wages, rents, or the cost of doing business.

There has not been adequate evidence of effectiveness of Fisk's model, but it is clear that individuals and groups do not interact on the basis of egoism or aggression; altruism or competition; fairness or cooperation. Yet, using the four categories appears to be an advantage to planning social change and sufficient as a starting point.

In the history of organizational management and societal change, with few exceptions, constructive change has been slow and in small increments over time. In most cases it was initiated by a small group with a strong leader who understood the environment sufficiently not to make an early mistake in calculating the resistance. Five areas normally respond to change: 1) individuals; 2) friends and family groups; 3) community and organizations; 4) the social order and financial matters; and 5) leadership and governance. The one constant in human life is change for better or worse.

It is more likely that individuals will first change, then groups. Groups are made up of individuals and when individuals change the group will change. As groups of people change, organizations and institutions change. As organizations and institutions change. governance is forced to change. This creates a change in leadership behavior or new leaders who accept the changes enter the picture. Change is the one constant in all human populations. When things are moving toward change it is the best time to influence the type of change that will be beneficial.

When the history of change is analyzed, a false positive often develops, that age and youthful vitality was the moving force for change. However, age and leader maturity are relative to a particular period of history or a unique situation such as war or a significant natural disaster. However, age and relative maturity are associated with historical circumstance. Leaders of history must be seen in the light of life expectancy: 25 during the Roman Empire; 33 by the Middle Ages; and reached 55 in the early 1900's. As life expectancy increased and leaders gained more experience, social change became less violent and more systematically controlled with more constructive outcomes.

In a multicultural society, religious conviction has a declining influence because of the variety of faith-based traditions; consequently, faith-based concerns are not the place to develop unity for a community effort toward positive social change. The starting place is humanitarian, because it is caring, compassionate, charitable and public-spirited. Why? Language and religion are the most deeply rooted aspect of culture.

Differences in religion are the most deeply rooted aspects of culture just below the attachment to the language of parents. This known as the "Mother Tongue" and is deeply engrained in the culture. Anything outside the faith or language of parents will be resisted. This is why language; family heritage and faith-based thinking are the three most difficult areas to produce constructive change in a multicultural community.

Those who seek to make changes in others have their own attachment to language, family heritage and faith. This is an obvious obstruction to initial movement toward change. The cultivation of friendship and the emphasis on common ground are the first steppingstones toward social change. The most workable place to begin positive social change is with preventable crime and immorality which impact children and families.

As individuals develop friendships and begin to learn to lessen the mistrust of others small changes will occur that include a personal reexamination of their ancestorial lifestyle and faith-based heritage. If there is a whisper that something is wrong with their faith-based practice of religion, or any derogatory remarks about language there will be an immediate hostile reaction. However, as individuals see beneficial change in other aspects of their life and community, they naturally become aware that their faith-based thinking is stuck in a "prison of previous patterns" and may not be entirely relevant to the present. This opens the door for the spiritual element to search the most essential part of an individual thinking.

23. LORD, search me and know my deepest reasoning, examine me and identify my most troubling beliefs. 24. Direct my thinking to anything which grieves you and guide me along the course of life to the future concealed from me. (Psalm 139:23-24 EDNT)

Those in charge must decide whether to behave as a catalyst or become a Change Agent. A catalyst may speed up change. but will not be changed in the process. This could be a serious drawback to full cooperation in any organized effort for constructive change. The members of a community expect the leadership group to grow, develop, and change over time. They also expect this change to be constructive. To remain the same and not change or fail to mature with the group creates a "left behind syndrome" and generates a reluctancy to act by others. This rush to action usually creates more difficulty than it solves. All action should be appropriately planned and understood behavior. There must be clearly expressed goals or reasons for all acts by leaders or citizens. Otherwise, the people will question the legitimacy of the behavior and chaos and disorder will follow.

On the other hand, when leaders behave as an Agent of Change, there is change on the part of the leader. As the situation changes and the people grow, the leader develops along with them. The concept of "team" is realized, and things get done in an efficient and effective manner. Consider Lewin's Force Field Theory Analysis. A situation audit is required as preparation.

What are the difficulties that must be overcome? How can the opposition be lessened? The force field construct reminds the leader that if only ten percent of the opposition can be removed it is the same as putting ten times the force forward for the cause, program, or project. With this in mind, all leaders should understand how to do a situation assessment. Less effort, time, and funds are required to move ten percent of the opposition than to increase ten times the force forward. To move equal and opposing forces a leader can take one of two approaches: (1) Increase the pressure ten times or, (2) concentrate on removing ten percent of the opposing forces. This is where the situation assessments aides in determining the best way forward.

There are seven steps in the situation assessment. One may better understand the concept and construct of the Situation Assessment by completing steps 1 -7 in a practice session. It is better to learn the procedure dealing with a hypothetical problem than to attempt a situation assessment later.

Do a Situation Assessment by completing 1-7

1. State where you are and where you want to be:
2. State all the forces that will assist you in making the desired change:
3. State all the forces that will hinder the making the desired change:
4. Analyze, prioritize and plot these forces on a grid
5. Brainstorm for possible "action strategy" options:
6. Select and further plan the best of these options:
7. Place the plan into the calendar.

Give yourself plenty of lead time for major change. Watch for excessive change in a short period.

Following a situational assessment where the proponents and opponents have been identified, there must be a process to change the attitude, or predisposition to act, of the respondents. To do this each individual must be classified as a radical, progressive, conservative or traditionalist in relationship to their attitude about change. Use the diagram below to assist your thinking about this issue.

Change Respondent Assessment

Proponents	Opponents

1		1
2		2
3		3
4		4
5		5

Remember, individuals change more rapidly than groups, and groups change faster than organizations. Concentrate on changing individuals. These changed individuals can slowly change the groups of which they are a part. As the groups change, the organization can move toward the cultural or social change that is required for the organization or institution to move forward.

Change Respondent Assessment can assist in planning a way forward. This way may be "over the hill and around the bend" but it is the only way to move a group, an organization, or change that is required to meet the present needs of the people and the organization.

Identify The Radicals	Identify The Progressives
Identify The Conservatives	Identify The Traditionalists

CLASSIFICATION OF CHANGE ATTITUDES			
Radicals	Progressives	Conservatives	Traditionalists

Who are they?

How will you deal with each group?

It is absolutely wrong to discriminate against an individual or group without cause. It is harmful to the total community for a few to express a prejudicial attitude or denigrate someone's race, culture, language, religion, or national background. Such behavior is based on adverse judgment or prejudice. Sacred writings are clear: *"God made of one blood all nations."* It is not only against the man's law; discrimination is morally evil and against God's law. Those who continually perpetrate such obscenities are often controlled by a hidden agenda expressed in overt discrimination.

Although such behavior is offensive to accepted standards of decency; it is tolerated by some who claim to be champions freedom and fairness. This is an abuse of tolerance and a counterfeit view of liberty. Such phony and prejudicial behavior must be continually challenged and ultimately overcome in order to effect constructive progress in social change.

Community politics often places individuals in office that oppose constructive social change. Individuals with good campaign slogans and solid resumes run for election with hidden motives. Instead of representing the needs of all the people; they concentrate on advancing the agenda of a few that financially support their election. Through these controlled politicians and a few misguided citizens, policies that would effect positive social changes are delayed or discarded. In this manner, political strong holds are created that hinder future social progress or at least slow the process to a "one step forward and two steps backward" so things stay about the same. This should never be acceptable in an informed society. It is time for a turn around.

> **Sidebar**: when my mother was a young teacher in a rural school on a cold and snowy day three young brothers were late for school. Mother asked for an explanation. It was a good one, *"Well, teacher it was so cold and slick out there every time we took a step toward school, we slid back two."* The follow up, *"Boys how did you ever get to school?"* The oldest boy answered firmly, ***"We got mad and started home!"*** Mother said she could not punish such a witty explanation.

Things never stay exactly the same; they usually will get worse. Perpetual discrimination and pervasive evil are established where constructive social change is hindered. These are areas where the political domain is inhabited by unethical individuals who are controlled by others who permit personal agendas to have total control over their attitudes. Remember, an attitude is a predisposition to act and this kind of attitude permits both inaction and artificial activity that is socially counterproductive. This attitude creates political crosscurrents and moral, ethical, and political conflict in the community. Doing nothing or disguising delaying strategy as "this is all we could get" is unacceptable. Evil triumphs when good people do nothing or permit others to squander legislative opportunities without being held accountable at the polls.

Doing nothing strengthens the strongholds of discrimination, favoritism, and bigotry by reaffirming the political views of reelected officials who failed to act in the first instance. There must be consequences at the polls for those who fritter away legislative opportunities or fail to do what they promised and were elected to do. Some call this political compromise, but "compromise" means *with-promise*. When individuals make campaign promises, such pledges must be kept or there should be consequences at the next election. Such negative activity creates a kind of political pretense of doing something when in fact the opposite has occurred.

Chapter Eight

ASSEMBLE
COMMUNITY ACTION GROUPS

Never neglect the experience which
produced the wisdom of the elderly.
During their trips around the sun
They witnessed God's Lighted pathway.
Daily they have learned the best way
up the Hill of Difficulty and
Through the valley of despair.
They learned from hardships and
Yearn for a better life for their children.
They can teach us these lessons.
We should listen!

A team approach where individuals offer part of the solution and in the end each one feels their contribution was the key that unlocked the dead bolt of the problem. A committee is often a false start, because it is provided with an agenda initiated by others. What is needed for workable social change is representative Action Groups which may function in two ways (1) as a *"think tank"* meeting to brainstorm about the need of the community and possible solutions or

(2) initiate *"barnstorming"* sessions as an informal meeting in a comfortable place with locals to get fresh and creative solutions directly from the people.

Action Groups should be representative of all parties that would be influenced by constructive change. Solutions up from the people are better received than suggestions coming down from outsiders. In a structured, yet free-thinking environment, the Action Group approach can best deal with antecedent causes of the problems instead of getting involved with problem people.

> **Sidebar:** on my first visit to Trinidad, it was surprising to hear the *"No problem"* response to almost every question. Over the next 15 years teaching at OASIS University Institute of Higher Learning and continuing to hear the same catch phrase "No problem!" There was a sign at a gas station "NP GAS" which I saw as no problem gas. It became obvious the phrase had nothing to do with gas or problems but was simply a colloquial or vernacular statement of the culture. However, one day my class was told of a planned book about Trinidad and asked for details. The title was *"The No-Problem People"* with a picture of the gas station sign on the cover. The books would have 12 chapters describing problems, but they would be called, Area of Concern One through Twelve. Why, "areas of concern" rather than listing problems? The "No Problem" people had only areas of concern. Identifying problems often names the person or persons believed to be the cause rather than the background situation which created the precursors of the present difficulties.

Why is expressing concern a better approach? Conditions and circumstances are much easier to discuss than the difficulties with people. In fact, certain people do actually cause part of the problem, but they are also part of the solution. To identify individuals as the cause alienates them from the process and half of the battle is already lost. An Action Group can freely process "brainstorming sessions" and discover possible conditions or causes and tailor discussion toward possible solutions without alienating individuals and their friends.

Why is dealing with antecedent causes rather than people a better approach to social change? Those who wish to have influence in a multicultural world must respectfully look for all signs of divine grace in the lives of those who follow a path different from the straight and narrow way taught to New Testament believers. The example of Jesus was clear, He was eager to recognize any evidence of faith outside His Galilean associates. In fact, all the original twelve (12) disciples were from Galilee and the 120 in the Upper Room were all acculturated Galileans, but the public that heard them speak asked, *"Are not all these who speak Galileans?"* (Acts 2) The early mission of faith was to cross all barriers to share divine love and grace. It becomes easy to hold others accountable when the accusers were not following the rules themselves. At an earlier time, Paul had a dispute with Peter and some Jews for their hypocrisy and trying to place Jewish restrictions on Paul's Gentile converts.

Before Peter's eyes were opened to share mercy and grace with Gentiles, he visited Paul at Antioch and attempted to place Gentile converts under Jewish restrictions which some Jews were not observing. Paul, being a former strict Pharisee, knew the Jewish law, customs and practices and saw that Jewish visitors were *"not walking uprightly according to the truth,"* or following the regulations of fellowship and visitation. Paul somewhat angrily clashed face to face with Peter in the presence of the others and said, "*I opposed him to his face, because he was wrong!*" Peter was later transformed by a vision in Joppa (Acts 10:9-22) into an early messenger to the Gentiles and a defender of redemptive grace reaching to them as it did to the Jewish people. *(Galatians 2:11-14)*

Peter was sent to the House of Cornelius and as he journeyed became hungry and fell into a trance and saw heaven open. This is when the door of grace was opened to others and Peter defended the gospel being preached to the Gentiles: he shared the events which prepared him to defend the extended move of grace to others.

> *... while they prepared a meal, he fell into a trance, 11. and saw heaven open and something like a sheet of sail cloth being let down to earth by ropes at the four corners: 12.* **it contained all manner of four-footed beasts and creeping and flying things.** *13. And a voice said,* **Rise, Peter; kill and eat.** *14. But Peter said,* **Not so Lord; for I have never eaten anything that is common or unclean.** *15. And the voice spoke again,* **What God had cleansed, you must not call defiled.** *(Acts 10:11-15 EDNT)*

> *6. The apostles and elders came together to consider the question. 7. After a heated discussion, Peter stood up and said, Brethren, you well know that in the past God made a choice that through my words the Gentiles should hear the gospel and learn to believe. 8. And God who knows the hearts of men, gave evidence of this by bestowing on them the Holy Spirit just as He did on us; 9. And God made no distinctions between*

*us and them by cleansing their hearts by faith.
(Acts 15:6-9 EDNT)*

It is obvious that many who follow a different faith-based path are deeply committed to all they have been taught by parents and religious leaders. They habitually follow the routine for prayers and participation in calendarized special days related to their faith. Jesus said, *"The learner is not above his teacher: but everyone who is fully taught will reach the level of his teacher." [sin is not reckoned where there is no law."]* **A loving and just God is more tolerant of those who follow what their faith taught them than those who do not behave what they were taught.**

Action groups are not appointed committees! They are by "invitation only" and create discussion and generate ideas for positive social change and community advancement! The Action Groups are small groups of seven (7) people interested in community change working with the Project Leader to bring information up from the people by encouraging creative thinking through "barnstorming" sessions. Each Action Group has a Leader and a Secretary and five (5) members. With seven (7) groups of seven (7) members working with the Project Leader; that is fifty (50) active thinking, praying, talking to each other about the needs of the community. Fifty (50) is the number of "harvest" or power in the Bible.

A Task Force of fifty (50) members

divided into seven Action Groups for community change; each group with seven members working with the Project Leader

ACTION GROUPS FOR COMMUNITY CHANGE

1. **Identify** local culture, language, and traditions.
2. **Recruit** interested parties to the cause of change.
3. **Communicate** the tasks in common language.
4. **Focus** all effort on community objectives and goals.
5. **Excite and direct** the self-activity of individuals.
6. **Facilitate** talking about both needs and solutions.
7. **Review and prioritize** all brainstorming ideas.

Seven (7) Action Groups prepared for Service

The Greeks used the word *homothumadon to express a* togetherness and strength meaning *"unanimously, with one mind, with one accord, at the same time."* There must be agreement and a willingness to work together. Since two are better than one; three must be better than two, and four are better than three, etc. This is why a small group of caring parents seeking God for understanding, knowledge and spiritual guidance may be able to construct a better future for their children. At least it is a start!

When Moses spoke concerning conditions for blessings, it was clear that five (5) could chase away 100 and 100 could cause 10,000 to flee. (Leviticus 26:8) Earlier at (25:22) Moses reminded the people that it took time to bring forth a new crop and that they would have to live by the stored food from the past until a new crop was harvested. Moses understood that the previously stored food was sufficient until a new crop grew. This is where social and faith-based groups are today: living on words and thoughts generated in the past, but a better crop will be available in the future provided the spiritual arithmetic is accepted: that is, five (5) * can influence 100 and the 100 can reach 10,000.

This is a "Together/Strong" endeavor that began with only five (5) kindred souls with the goal of influencing 100 with the fresh crop (of ideas). The 100 can use the ideas generated by the Action Groups to influence the larger group *[in the Leviticus plan the 100 could deal with 10,000 and bring safety and progress to the population.]*

> **Sidebar:** Example of a **Together/Strong Action Group** which became a Task Force... *In 1974 five (5) mature individuals were chosen as a working group to determine how we could change the world in our lifetime. After several weeks of prayer and planning, it was decided we needed a Task Force of 100 to accomplish the objective. A Society of Scholars was structured to do research and seven years later (1981) fifty-seven of the original 100 convened in Tennessee to launch Oxford Graduate School with the goal of creating World Changers. Forty-years later several hundred God-called men and women have graduated with master's and doctorates and become part of the Scholars doing social research for the sociological integration of religion and society to change the world.*

Using the Greek construct of togetherness embodied in *homothumadon*, the concern is directed toward assisting social faith-based groups to work *with one mind, with one accord, at the same time."* to find ways and means to navigate a pathway through the existing multicultural maze and restore the basic principle of unity among the People of God. How can the barriers of culture, tradition, habits, and language be overcome to construct a platform where all faith-based groups can share the message of Divine love and Redeeming grace? The Lord is long-suffering toward the human race and not willing for anyone to perish but that all find their way to repentance. A quality repentance is accompanied by Godly sorrow for past behavior.

> *Therefore, my dearly beloved, as you were always obedient, keep on working out the deliverance of the congregation with a humble frame of mind.* **For it is God working in you to make you both willing and able to do His good pleasure.** **Do all things without grumbling and disagreements:** *that you may be above suspicion and unblemished, the children of God, with an untarnished reputation, in the midst of a warped and twisted nation, where you shine as lights in the world; holding forth the word of life...* (Philippians 2;12-16A EDNT)

What specific problems do faith-based groups face in their attempt to communicate a common message of love and grace in a multicultural environment? Years of confusing traditions, cultural rules and dominant voices protecting the past regardless of the cost to the present and the future. This *"freeze-frame thinking"* can only be overcome through prayer, research and academic excellence to demonstrate ways to communicate the message of God's love to a troubled world. Just as individuals are redeemed and brought into the Family of God one at a time, each faith-based group must become part of a "Together/Strong" force willing to support constructive change in a multi-cultural community for the benefit of their family and a better future for all concerned.

Obviously, a working group may get too large with many voices to work effectively in a constrained situation. Remember, Gideon's force of 32,000 was reduced to

300 hand-picked individuals with a specific task. Small, but acting together with clear spiritual guidance, they were strong enough for a positive outcome but small enough for God to have the credit for the victory. (Judges 6&7) Never look down on small numbers when fighting a spiritual battle. Where two or three are gathered in focused faith the Power of God is there.

Perhaps the founders of the USA were wise in establishing the Electoral College, limiting the Supreme Court, and restricting two Senators for each state. As well as requiring a population count to establish a Congressional Representative's accountability. This is true representative governance! Sacred scripture early warned *Israel not to follow a multitude to do evil;* (Exodus 23:2)

Never neglect the wisdom of mothers. Remember, before there were institutions of higher learning, mothers prepared their children to rule the world. Always include mothers in structuring Action Groups and the Together/Strong NETWORK. A true event may assist in establishing the value of a mother's prayer supported words.

> **Sidebar:** In my last pastorate before I entered full-time into academia, it was my privilege to accept a call to a rural congregation who worshiped in an old chapel of a burned-out Congregational Teachers' College. The urgent need, beyond reaching the men of the community, was to build a new building. It took seven years to build a beautiful brick place for worship without a debt. After dedication day the question arose, *"Who will have a key to the building?"*
>
> The Trustees, because of their sweat equity wanted only the active trustees to have a key. The Deacons were willing for all the donors to the building fund

to have a key. Neither option was acceptable. The item was tabled until the next Business Meeting with a request that each one pray about the matter. The next meeting the standoff remained so the matter was delayed to the next meeting. There was no chance for consensus.

This process was unacceptable to me and a few others who considered the security of the building in a rural area with so many keys. A church had been built without a squabble, now a little brass key was dividing the whole congregation. That is until an elderly mother spoke up, *"Preacher they ain't prayed a lick. I prayed and believe God gave me a solution: Brother Donnie is a Trustee, and he operates a store across the street from the church. Why don't we put a key in his cash register and if anyone needs to enter the building between services it would be convenient for them to get a key and sign and return it. Then we would have a record of who entered and why."*

The congregation agreed and for 90 days no one asked for a key to enter the church. An elderly lady who thought her usefulness was over, through prayer and wisdom, found an answer to a problem that was doing great harm to the fellowship. *God bless the praying women and cause the men to listen to their wisdom!*

The Divine Nurturing Attribute, as part of the DNA of females, blossoms to maturity with the onset of motherhood. A mother's affection for her offspring is almost unfathomable by others. The news of the world chronicles their heroic concern almost daily. The prudent goodwill of mothers is universally known. First by personal observation of our own mothers; then by what some call the "good sense of mothers." The time used to observe the forethought and discretion used by mothers in the care and control of their children is an experiential lesson not found in books. It is wise to learn from individuals who have birthed and cared for a child.

The predisposition for nurturing behavior of mothers is akin to *agape "one-way love"* with which God loves us all. Those who are not biological parents also have a touch of this nurturing attribute. Also, the experience of mature fathers is a reservoir of valuable knowledge for positive human interaction. Maturity breeds confidence as well as knowledge and a desire to assist others. Valuable lessons may also be learned from mature fathers.

Paul had a good dose of DNA – Divine Nurturing Attribute in (1 Thessalonians 2) vs 7-8 Paul explained his maternal and paternal feelings and expressed a kind motherly-love for his converts. Then in vs. 11-12 he clearly behaved as a father encouraging, comforting and charging his converts to lead a life worthy of God's high calling.

> ***But we were tender among you, even as a nursing mother warmly takes pleasure in her children: 8. so affectionately longing for you, we were willing to share with you, not only the gospel of God, but also well-pleased to share our lives, because you were valued by us***. *9. You remember our long and hard labor night and day, because we would not burden you for expenses, but freely preached the gospel of God unto you. 10. You are witnesses and so is God, how upright, honest and blameless was our conduct among you that believe: 11.* **as you know how we encouraged, comforted, and charged every one of you, as a father treats his children***, 12. that you would lead a life worthy of God, who has called you unto the glory of His kingdom. (1Thessalonians 1:7-12 EDNT)*

The place to start for positive social and/or spiritual change in a multicultural community is with mature parents and their God-like DNA -Divine Nurturing Attribute desiring their children and grandchildren to have a better future. Such individuals gathering for curative prayer is the path to constructive change in both thought and behavior in dealing with most human problems. Never overlook the experience gained by parenting children. Parent's influence hopes and dreams for their children outweighs silver and gold.

Meditation and reflection in prayer is effectual and fervent intercession for others. Common behavior in the three monotheistic religions: Judaism, Christianity and Islam are private and public prayers. Monotheism has the common ground of accepting the One and Only God, Creator and Sustainer of the Universe and normally direct their prayers based on the belief that there is only One God. This is firm common ground for cooperation in spiritual matters provided those who faithfully offer prayers also listen for and follows Divine guidance.

Differences divide and often conceal the common ground that could bring unity of effort in overcoming generations of background heritage. This could enable the fulfilling of basic human needs: food, shelter and safety ought to be the common goals for all who worship the One and only God, Creator and Sustainer of the Universe regardless of the designated identity of the Supreme Deity they worship. It is self-evident that all who serve one God should be working together to provide for the advancement and common good t of the People of God. Unless the process is encumbered by the selfishness of the human heart or impeded by organized religion which obstruct the righteous cause of the Creator? Most faith-based groups have divisions and dogma which limit their global effectiveness. Each group behaves as if they have found the "Holy Grail" and have exclusive access to the "secrets" of an afterlife.

A generic least common denominator social or faith-based structure is not the answer, there must be an approach to change operations sufficiently to be acceptable by all concerned. The principle of *"One God-One Faith"* is the common ground upon which to establish a plan to "*reach the reachable and teach the teachable in order to win the winnable,*" because God is longsuffering and "*not willing that any should perish but that all take the path to repentance." (2 Peter 3:9)* The Greek for repentance suggest the need for sufficient "quality" to enable a "turnaround" in lifestyle behavior.

Prayer and a devotional heart of love for God becomes common ground for cooperation in social change for the benefit of family and children. There are other areas of similarities in the three monotheistic religions: attitudes of sacrifice, good works, hospitality, peace, justice, journey to a shrine or sacred place, and an afterlife. To become progressive in engendering cooperation among multicultural people is to seek for similarities rather than differences.

Commonalities unite where any differences divide and become a deal breaker. This is partly true because most see compromise as being negative when in reality it is an agreed contract when two parties "promise" to work together in certain areas to reach a commonly desired objective. This is a "spiritual" area where Divine assistance and human maturity are required. One simple fact is true: *"If the difference does not change*

the population of heaven or the number with a positive
afterlife, is it really a reason for division?"

There is hope for a moral and faith-based agenda
that could change a community one person and one
group at a time. In the case of early Christianity, it would
be good to note that all places of worship were identified
by location not by doctrine. Such common ground must
be self-evident to the people without ecclesiastical
validation. This could remove most of the hostility and
open the gates in the dividing walls for free passage.
Notwithstanding the limits of common ground, moral
and spiritual leaders must find a starting place and
move slowly and surely forward. Overcoming problems
and fulfilling basic human needs should be the concern
of all who honor and worship the One and Only God,
Creator and Sustainer of the Universe. Such an effort
could restore the "One God-One Faith" to the common
experience of the human race provided the faith-based
teaching was stripped of man-made components and
retained the common elements that advances the worth-
ship of God in all aspects of life. This could change many
differences and promote unity.

God is not dead! Religion did not face away as an
old soldier. The predictions concerning the early demise
of faith were premature. None of the secular prophets
were correct. Although attendance has declined, a
basic belief in God remains deep in the human psychic.
What is missing is a genuine togetherness and common
agreement for being a moral citizen of the community and
a mystical citizen of heaven.

The only hope for a viable monotheistic, faith-based
movement and witness is an internal redirection of the

heart and soul that brings with it a moral lifestyle and resistance to the immorality of society. Such redirection could bring both a commitment to the common tenets of sacred history and a spirit of teamwork among people of faith. A change in the standard "religious rhetoric" could break the barriers of "freeze framed thinking," and "name brand religion" and make One Lord -- One Faith meaningful again. According to sacred history, all three monotheistic faiths were in agreement as to the need for unity among themselves: what is needed now is a sense of cooperation among monotheistic believers.

> **The words of the Qur'an:** *Let there, arise out of you one community, inviting to all that is good, enjoining what is right, and forbidding what is wrong: those will be themselves and fall into disputations after receiving clear signs: for them is a dreadful penalty (Qur'an 3:105).*

> **The words David**: *Behold, how good and pleasant it is when brothers dwell in unity! (Psalms 133:1).*

> **The words of Jesus:** *"A kingdom divided is brought to destruction; and a house divided falls." (Luke 11:17).*

Judaism honors Jehovah but is a diverse religion and members hold a variety of beliefs and interpretations of Jewish law and practice. The main divisions are: Orthodox, Reform, and Conservative. Yet, Jews share a common core of beliefs and would feel at home in any Synagogue around the world. The Book of Chronicles is a brief Hebrew history and contains a primary challenge to penitence and restoration of spiritual foundations.

> *If my people, which are called by my name, shall humble themselves, and pray, and seek my face,*

and turn from their wicked ways; then will I hear from heaven, and will forgive their sin, and will heal their land. (2 Chronicles 7:14)

Christianity honors Jesus but is divided into Catholic and Protestant. Protestantism has more than 300 divisions with multiple differences in doctrine. The central disagreements dishonor Jesus and the early spiritual leadership. Peter, considered the first leader of the Way, wrote a general letter to scattered believers suffering from religious persecution and emphasized that Messiah-like behavior was needed to correct the inferior aspects of a community before a superior foundation of faith could be constructed that would unify the message of grace to the world. The words of Peter speak to the central construct of this book:

*8. Finally, you must think the same thoughts, share difficulties with one another, having automatic inter-dependence with brotherly kindness; be tender-hearted and humble-minded: 9. you must not repay injury with injury, or hard words with hard words, but bless those who curse you. **For you were called to give kind words to others and come to a well-spoken eulogy at the end.** 10. For the one wishing to love life and see prosperous days, let him avoid an evil tongue and cunning words. 11. Habitually avoid evil and do good things; let him seek and follow peace. 12. Because the eyes of the Lord watch over the righteous, and his ears listen to their prayers: but the Lord looks directly into the eyes of wrongdoers.* (1 Peter 3:8-12 EDNT)

Islam honors Allah but has partitions that divide the people who submit to God. The largest divisions are the Sunnis and Shi'ites. Sunni Islam is the dominant sect worldwide. Shiite Islam is the dominant sect in Iran and the surrounding area. A third division is Ibadi Islam the dominant sect in Oman. There are others in spite of The Prophets admonition to avoid division:

> *And hold fast, all together, by the rope which Allah (stretches out for you) and be not divided among yourselves; and remember with gratitude Allah's favor on you; for ye were enemies and He joined your hearts in love, so that by His Grace, ye became brethren; and ye were on the brink of the pit of Fire, and He saved you from it. Thus, doth Allah make His Signs clear to you: That ye may be guided?* (Qur'an 3:103)

A single group will never restore morality or feed all the children or care for the sick and dying. One group alone cannot eliminate poverty, violence, human and drug trafficking or complete the task of global constructive change. A common agenda must be established to first make people moral citizens of the world before they can become mystical citizens of heaven. Remember, the goal for spiritual outreach is not dominance or control, but emancipation of the family from poverty and violence and to provide liberty to individuals to choose their way of life and eternal destiny at the hands of Providence. For this to happen, the barriers to personal expressions of faith must be torn down. Where there is common ground the monotheistic religions should cooperate at least in the areas of humanitarian projects, crime prevention and the control of unbridled morality that brings great harm to children and families. Since prayers are made to the same God, perhaps a common prayer agenda would be a start. All families, communities and people have common needs, hopes and fears: could there not be a prayer agenda that include these common areas of concert.

> **Sidebar:** In 1981 A Task Force chartered a Graduate Program offering a Doctor of Philosophy in the sociological integration of religion and society. The students from many countries and faith-based groups made up early classes. They came from Armenia, Australia, Canadian, China, Costa Rica, Denmark, Egypt, Formosa (ROC), Germany, Haiti, India, Italy, Jamaica, Japan, Kenya, Liberia, Nigeria, Palestine, Philippians, S. Africa, Saint Kitt, Singapore, Trinidad, UK, Ukraine, USA, USVI, and Vietnam. This represented many cultures, traditions, and faith-based groups. Since the program dealt with integration in a safe atmosphere to study, three concerns were anticipated: 1) a diversity in the classroom; 2) common music for the Chapel; 3) a pristine approach to communion that would not hinder participation.

1. How would we deal with gender, race, language and religion in the classroom? The decision was to have no more than two students of the same denomination or faith-based group in same class. This would enable individuals to freely discuss and not fear that someone would feel they were disloyal to their tradition.

2. Since music is an expression of culture, how would we find music that the diverse groups knew. A musician was asked to find a common or well-known tune with different words. He found the lyrics by Matthew Bridges (1848) "My God Accept My Heart" that was compatible with tune Amazing Grace.

3. A group was asked to write a generic script for Holy Communion stripped of denominational language as near the oldest historic record they could find. The best three were selected and used in Chapel. Then the three were taken together

and edited into a fresh script to be used at Chapel Communion. The Choice was to use One Loaf of Bread and One Chalice for grape juice, using an early Intinction method where each person served themselves by breaking a piece of bread and dipping into the juice. Seventy-two faith-based groups have participated in Chapel Communion. At some large academic functions, a generic prayer of the Chalice was used in an element-less communion.

My God Accept My Heart

Matthew Bridges: 1848   Tune: Amazing Grace

My God, accept my heart this day,
And make it always thine,
That I from thee no more may stray,
No more from thee decline.

Anoint me with thy heavenly grace,
And seal me for thine own,
That I may see thy glorious face,
And worship near thy throne.

Before the cross of Him who died,
Behold, I prostrate fall.
Let every sin be crucified,
And Christ be all i all.

Let every thought and work and word,
To thee be ever given,
Then life shall be thy service, Lord,
And death the gate of heaven.

AMEN!

Most faith-based groups are more interested in their specific dogma and polity than connecting with the local community. Organized religion fails to join the interest or purpose of the people of a particular locale. Always some higher, more pressing agenda imposes both method and message on the people rather than meeting the needs of the community. Local congregations seem to have no partnership, no walking together or joining forces to meet the goals of the people. Protestant congregations require the people to adapt to the program of the church, whether it meets their needs or not.

Do you have a personal stake in the outcome of constructive change? Are you transparent concerning your interest? Do you understand the complexity of the community and the positive and negative aspects of a multicultural environment? If the objectives of beneficial change are reached, what percentage of the community will benefit? Will you be able to assemble Action Groups to secure sufficient information from the people to proceed? Are the community leaders known? Has the proponents and opponents of change been identified for this community?

Missional living is working together with God in advancing the message of love-mercy-grace to the world. Wisdom brings authenticity and genuineness to the daily lives of those desiring a missional lifestyle. In faith-based thinking *missional living is the adoption of the attitude, thinking, behaviors, and practices of a missionary in order to engage others in the process of advancing the gospel message.* Wisdom speaks further to the faithful who attend with interest to instruction and are blessed by keeping to the proper pathway. There is a warning not to disregard the lessons learned.

Those who listen and are watchful daily at the open door of wisdom will find life and favor from the Lord and will enjoy a missional reality. This is the day for fellowship among the band of believers, time for full commitment to the kingdom of God. After leaving Thessalonica, Paul journeyed to Corinth. Later he wrote the believes at Corinth about working together with God to advance the gospel. He basically told them *"God is working; you must get together."*

> 8.*He who did the planting and the one doing the watering are part of the same process: and every man will receive a reward according to his work. 9.* **For God is working and the laborers are together:** *you are God's farm you are God's field to be worked and God's building to be constructed. 10. According to the favor of God given to me, as a wise master builder,* **I have laid a foundation, and another will build on it. But let every worker take heed how he builds on the foundation. 11. There is no other foundation for the building but the one laid on Jesus Christ.** (I Corinthians 3:8-11 EDNT)

Missional behavior is adopting the thinking, behaviors, and practices of a missionary in order to globalize the gospel.

There is a missional reality that supports a lifestyle! Essentially, a missional reality coalesces around a personalized grasp of scripture that offers a theological shift, a sociological direction, and a distinct lifestyle for believers. The missional mindset is placed in the context of viewing the Cross through the Empty Tomb, seeing culture as a vehicle of communication, the church as a force to work with not of a field in which to work, because the community and the world is a mission field ready for harvest. Sadly, the workers are few!

What does a missionary know and how do they feel about the lost world? They know beyond a doubt they have been called to serve outside their comfort zone. They understand they must leave family and friends and travel into a strange land. They are aware of the new language and culture they will face. Called and appointed Missionaries know they must live a life worthy of financial and prayerful support from an extended constituency. They know they have limited resources and that through deputation they must raise replace funds for what is spent, or they cannot continue their work. This provides a missionary family a totally different perspective on money matters than a state side family involved in ministry. A family involved in missions cultivates a positive mindset that God is in charge of their lives and ministry. Missionaries must teach their children to live on a limited budget and that every cent saved enhances their chance of winning a soul for Christ. In fact, the missionary and their lifestyle are often lonely and full of daily difficulties. Without safe living quarters, clean sheets on the bed, good food on the table, and with only local native people protecting them against hostile forces, missionary families develop an uncertain way of life. Can we say, *"God bless the missionaries!"* Then in the next breath say, **"Lord help me to walk the right pathway and demonstrate a missional lifestyle to others and be supportive of those called to serve overseas."**

A missionary's work is hard and often harsh, and it is even more difficult for their family. The convenience of a well-furnished home, good schools for the children, and a well-stocked food market, good transportation, and interstate highways for rapid movement are nowhere to be found in most places where missionaries life and work. Recently, by oldest son, Barton, had an opportunity to visit Guatemala for few days. He thought he was going to sing, pray and listen to missionaries speak. Traveling on a mountain road to an isolated village, to his surprise, he was handed a hammer and told *"We are building houses this week."* Another surprise, they were building on the side of a volcano (which erupted a few days later and killed many). In the past he had complained about my mile-long road up Lone Mountain to my retirement compound, but after this new experience he sent a message, *"Tell Dad he has a wonderful road up his mountain."* It would be great if every overweight, over paid member of a faith-based congregation could spend a week on a primitive mission field. Most likely they would return with a changed attitude, as one of my previous members did: he prayed after returning, *"Lord, I will freely support those missionaries, but please don't ask me to live and work there."* It is relatively easy to take a "mission trip" with a group of excited believers but living and working in the same austere and bleak environment over time is a different story.

> 8. Finally, you must think the same thoughts, share difficulties with one another, having automatic interdependence with brotherly kindness; be tender-hearted and humble-minded: 9. you must not repay injury with injury, or hard words with hard words, but bless those who curse you. For

*you were called to give kind words to others
and come to a well-spoken eulogy at the end.*
10. **For the one wishing to love life and see
prosperous days, let him avoid an evil tongue
and cunning words. 11. Habitually avoid evil
and do-good things; let him seek and follow
peace. 12. Because the eyes of the Lord watch
over the righteous, and His ears listen to their
payers:** *but the Lord looks directly into the eyes of
wrongdoers. (1 Peter 3:8-12 EDNT)*

When a link breaks the chain is made shorter; it may reach to Jerusalem, Judea, and Samaria, but may not be long enough to reach the farthest part of the earth. The Challenge of Jesus and the reason Jesus asked the Father to send the Holy Spirit was to bring the disciples miraculous ability and strength to follow the instructions and stay on course for the distance. If the world is to be reached with the love of God and the lessons of grace, the message must be protected by strengthening the weak links in the chain of outreach.

The missionary challenge was to reach the uttermost part of the earth, not to pick and choose the close or the easiest places, but the mandate was *"as you go into all the world make disciples."* To make disciples, converts must be identified with the Trinity through baptisms, and taught all that Jesus began to teach from the beginning of His ministry until the Ascension. This is why local Faith-based groups must accept this challenge, have a nonsectarian worldview and strengthen the weak links in the chain of missionary outreach. This is true missionary support. Missions needs people as well as funds to complete the journey on the road less traveled. The end is worth the journey.

16. the Holy Spirit joins with our human spirit confirming that we are the children of God: 17. since we are children, then heirs, and fellow-heirs with Christ; if we suffer together, we may also be glorified together. 18. **For I consider the sufferings we now endure not worthy to be compared with the glory about to be revealed in us. 19.** *All creation is yearning expecting to see the appearance of the children of God. (Romans 8:16-19 EDNT)*

Sidebar: The Book of Acts has no close; it is assumed that Luke planned to write a third book on the extension of God's love and the lessons of grace. Perhaps the Holy Spirit left that work to the generation before the return of Jesus. What has your faith-based group done lately?

A viable faith-based message requires an
internal redirection of the heart and soul
of all who claim the moral high ground.
This would bring with it a personal
commitment to the common principles of
the moral and sacred essentials,
spirit of cooperation with less division
and eliminate the barriers of
"culturally named worship" and
the "freeze-frame thinking."

Chapter Nine

AMEND
FREEZE-FRAME THINKING

Freeze-frame is a process for stopping the action to focus more closely on a single frame. Before modern technology, a photographer took twelve camera shots of a galloping horse to win a bet that there were times when all four hooves were off the ground. The process is now used in sports, movies, news, photography or viewing a security camera tape in an investigation. There are many names and uses for the process: still frame, single shot, still picture, etc. In 2015, Brian Hedden expanded the freeze-frame process to conceptualize a "time-slice" discussion of rational and irrational behavior.

This book attempts to view ancestral heritage, culture, tradition, and faith-based behavior as being influenced by a slice of time in the past that creates "freeze-frame" thinking. The bonding glue of the past controls much of current behavior. The assumption is that long-term recall of family, early educators, and faith-based pedagogical guidance has the capacity to influence cognitive and affective decision-making into adulthood. Such "freeze-frame" thinking complicates positive social change. It appears that many individuals and groups hold on to the past with a tenacity which breeds resistance to even the natural growth that comes with experience, maturity, and environmental changes.

My personal experience with this obstinacy and wrongheadedness used to break fellowship and relationships over trivial matters has been a troubling factor in efforts to be a change agent in matters of education, equal rights, positive social change and the integration of faith-based behavior into civil society. Traveling and speaking in 105 counties, writing 50 + books dealing with the need for social and spiritual change, justice and equality has made only small incremental changes in the lives of a few.

Navigating Multiculturalism –Challenges for Faith-based Groups, is part of my legacy to influence constructive change for the sake of liberty and justice for all, a moral lifestyle based on relevant faith-based principles, and cooperation among monotheistic believers for a common agenda to enable individuals to become moral citizens of society in the process of becoming mystical citizens of heaven.

The worship of the One and only True God, Creator and Sustainer of the Universe has become many culturally identified groups with dogmatic leaders, competing agendas, and opposing methodologies. Leaders should take the initiative to bring renewal and restoration to the faith-based movements and make love and grace central to the global mission. Faith-based leaders must reach beyond their homogeneous group, gathered in a culturally inspired sanctuary, in a concerted effort to benefit a multicultural society.

Since positive change takes place at the level of ideas and values, ideology is the common ground for constructing positive change in an organization. Philosophy and theology combine to create ideology and identity. This is where values, ideas and social roles come together. Often the constituency with strong leaders are stuck in a prison of previous patterns, a kind of freeze-frame thinking based on slices of time in the past. It is precisely which requires a transparent openness when communicating the justification for needed change. Most individuals are comfortable when the past overlaps the present and contains elements relevant to their comfort zone. This is why leadership must be aware of all the constituency and publics of their organization to influence any constructive change.

Sidebar: reminded of an incident in Oxford, UK in the early 1960's. After considerable time in the "religion" section of a large used bookstore, seven (7) books were selected. Presenting them to the gray-haired gentleman at the counter, I was surprised, even shocked at his questions and comments. He asked, "Are you an American?" My answer was in the affirmative. He then asked, "Are you a member of the cloth?" Declaring myself a member of the clergy, I listened to the gentleman's plea, *"Please don't take these books to America. They have already emptied the churches in England!"* Out of respect for his wisdom and sincerity, I left the books on the counter and walked out into the cold air of reality. Grateful for the English gentlemen's insight, since that time I have been cautious about picking anything out of another language, culture, or time period and expecting it to work adequately under the present circumstance.

The best hope for beneficial change among moral and faith-based People is an internal redirection of mind, heart and soul. The mind controls *awareness* of the past which influences the present, the heart is the core of *emotional attachment* to the past which holds on to concepts which resist change, and the soul is the God-breathed part of man where moral corruption and worthless behavior *conflicts* with a teachable faith-based spirit that could firmly establish the spiritual part of man that determines all behavior. Since the New Testament was recorded mostly in *koine* Greek, this writer prefers the Greek understanding of a God-breathed soul or *psyche,* as the moral rationale of a human being: character, consciousness, feeling, perception, reasoning and unscrambling options. Understanding this process is prerequisite to beneficial social change.

This would bring with it a personal commitment to basic moral principles without cultural clothes or traditions with no relevance to the present. With this there must be a teachable spirit and cooperation with a lessening of mistrust as the barriers of "culturally identified behavior" controlled by "freeze-thinking" is made relevant to current needs. Many rituals and practiced traditions used in the past had good foundations for the time and situation, but many were based on fear rather than on moral issues. Changes in the moral DNA -Divine Nurturing Attribute that was instructive in a common culture will no longer work in a multicultural society. The list is too long to add here, but a few obvious ones will illustrate the reasons some things no longer work.

Consider that the past behavioral guidance was based on fear rather than on moral principles which guide ethics and decency. This would be considered negative by reasonable people or more recently seen as reverse psychology which caused the young to search for ways around the rules. Coaching based on moral and ethical guidance for respect and civility would be considered positive. A proposition that is positive implies a negative which is undesirably, harmful and destructive.

Look at the historical advice on sexual promiscuity: it was based on the fear of pregnancy, an incurable disease and the embarrassment of self and family rather than on morality. In the past each sexual encounter was subject to pregnancy or some sexually transmitted disease which would place limitations on individuals. Presently, with prophylactics, birth control pills, and high-powered medicines to cure STD's, those threats have been removed. With these social changes came free-love, rampant sexual misconduct, when the only real prevention of sexual promiscuity is morality, respect for others and responsibility for behavior. When science or personal cleverness can circumvent the previous disastrous results, respect and morality guidance may lessen the fallout and restore some civility. How, when and where would such an approach begin in the change timetable?

The purpose of gender difference must be taught to the young: perhaps as early as ages 6 to 9, boys and girls ought to be taught to be respectful of gender difference and understand their future role as parents. The female was designed to become a wife and a mother and ought to be guided by this understanding. Males were made to be husbands and fathers. We teach the young to respect parents, siblings and other blood-relatives and even the "girl next door." However, the explosion of sexual promiscuity has lost the special value of gender. This has created a progressive and shameless violation of the human anatomy and survival. Many fear the change in sexual proximity is permanent and the Arabian idiom about the *"genie getting out of the bottle"* has become true-to-life reality. Perhaps civil society is on a slippery slope toward the mindset of Sodom and Gomorrah. It has become clear that some permissive behavior and changes are not relevant to a moral lifestyle or social atmosphere for conceiving, birthing and nurturing the next generation as moral citizens of the world.

A simplification of faith-based worship and more clear examples of "a behavioral lifestyle" which becomes a moral pattern for others is the starting point of positive social change. A living-breathing-behaving human example is similar to a picture being worth 1,000 words of a Pastor's homily. Present society has only political or sports heroes for the young to follow. Can you name three faith-based heroes from your place of worship whose daily lifestyle behavior would be instructive of a moral life and a faith-based family?

The three Abrahamic religions: Judaism, Christianity and Islam worship the One and only True God, Creator and Sustainer of the Universe. It appears that many reduce the Creator God to a higher power, supreme authority, superior force majeure and force greater than self. It appears that the term Higher Power is used by Alcohol Anonymous (AA) to identify a power greater than self to refer to a supreme being or deity or other conceptions of God. This group is not a religious organization but seem to be using God's Power to produce social change more than most faith-based operations.

Historic faith-based entities have become culturally identified groups with sectarian positions, competing agendas, and opposing methodologies. The influence of ancestral heritage, language and culture are so firmly established that leadership is only working to maintain the *present state of affairs and the way things stand.* This means nothing changes and all have become comfortable and no one is willing to "rock the boat" or initiate a small modification or adjust a minor variation in the *status quo.* Of course, the Abrahamic religions are old and rigid and those who manage affairs of faith are satisfied with things as they are, and comfortable leaders dare not risk opposing ecclesial authority.

> **Sidebar:** I am reminded of an excellent Greek scholar in one of my graduate courses who also pastored a great church. His denomination required an annual renewal of credentials Should a clergy change his belief even slightly it had to be reported on the annual renewal form. This Greek scholar began to change his perception of *"eternal vs. everlasting"* and wrote a lengthy document explaining this change and that it would not influence his pulpit preaching. He vowed not to speak publicly anything that disagreed with the denominational position. Yet, his credentials were not renewed, and he lost his pulpit. This incident caused a good church to lose a great pastor and the local University to gain an excellent professor. This example shows why local ministers are slow to think, speak or write anything different from the standard dogma of their congregation. Consequently, faith-based groups are not an effective instrument of social change. Social change must start with individuals.

Authors, academics, theologians and learned professionals must take the initiative to bring renewal and restoration to the historic faith-based movements and make lifestyle changes central to the faith-based global mission. Yes, faith-based people can love the sinner but hate the sin! What is the difference between a gross sinner and a "so called" godly saint? The simple answer is a changed "behavioral lifestyle." A more complex answer from theology is the act of believing and accepting God's redemptive treatment which eliminates guilt and the power of habitual behavior over human nature. Has God's willingness changed that *none should perish but that all should participate in a change of sufficient quality to influence their behavioral lifestyle?*

Sidebar: When a member of my pastorate was facing a potentially fatal operation he was asked about his current relationship with God. His surprise response, "Pastor, I was baptized and joined the church as a teenager, but it didn't take." When asked for further explanation he reacted, *"It's like a vaccination that didn't leave a mark on your arm and had to be done over. I guess it was never done over."* We prayed for his assurance of salvation. It was Wednesday evening. He was dead by Friday afternoon. This reminds me of an old country preacher who said, *"If being born again didn't change your life...try being born again!"*

All must be welcome in the places of worship regardless of when, where, or who is attending. Each genuine profession of faith is accepted by God whether it follows mine or your scared tradition of "Ole Time Religion." Faith-based groups must reach beyond the walls of a culturally identified sanctuary to the multicultural human race with a message of grace. Why? *God is not willing that any should parish... but desires all to take the way of personal change.* (2 Peter 3:9)

*24. The God who ordered the universe and all the things in it, the One being Lord of heaven and earth does not dwell in hand made shrines; 25. neither is He served by human hands, as though He needed something from man, **seeing He gives to all life, breath, and all things; 26. and has made of one blood all nations of men who dwell on the earth, determined the history of nations and their territory; 27. so they should search for God and hopefully find Him although He is not far from all of us. 28. For in Him we live and move, and have our being;*** (Acts 17:24-28a EDNT)

A period of history created the framework for culturally branded faith systems in different parts of the world. Because of the culturally different period of time each system has distinctive differences which sets it apart from all others. Even the three Abrahamic entities have drastic differences with one commonality: all are built on a monotheistic faith with multiple culturally based behaviors and traditions. Each of the three have divisions and sub-divisions. These three have some commonalities and many differences based on culture.

The most critical division among all faith-based groups is the primary idea of exclusivity and that all others have a false foundation and a corrupt basis for teaching and distorted and partisan lifestyle. It is for these reasons that exclude other faiths from "True religion" that causes many to think they are not worthy of respect. Differences divide and the multiplicity of disparities, divergences, and discrepancies which breeds disputes and disagreements creates disrespect between groups and complicates most efforts for constructive social change in communities, townships, cities and municipalities.

This precipitated a brand identity for local places of worship clothed in cultural clothes with a sectarian bias. Over generations freeze-frame thinking stubbornly maintained much of the original focus with complete disregard for the cultural threads with which it was woven innocence or the social changes in a multicultural society. Perhaps only a divine change of heart and mind clothed the nakedness of Adam and Eve. Even the average person understands the difference in clothing in a hot climate as opposed to a cold climate. If a very cold climate or an extremely hot climate attempted to establish a common dress code for all faith-based people, it would be unenforceable. Why? Because weather creates part of the cultural traditions of people.

> **Sidebar:** my travels have taken me to over 100 countries and my ministry has included 72 denominations or faith-based groups. It was shocking to see drastic differences in the expected behavior of church-folk in different cultures.

Faith development over time was based on writings from a slice of time in a particular culture and language. Through the years, faith-based thinking was frozen in the past and lacks adequate relevance to the present global ethos. Most faith-based thinkers stopped the action of their theological clock at a particular time in history.   The concepts and constructs of individual thinkers were lifted from a cultural context in the past and placed into the complex and multicultural global scene. Each separate township, rural community, urban metropolis has become part of a global village connected by multiple communication platforms. Each child and whole families are bombarded with mixed messages and opinionated reports of every negative thing that happens in the world.

This overload of "bad news" may be part of the deaf ear syndrome that has tuned out any faith-based good news. It seems that the high-tech world has placed a foghorn funnel in the public ear and filed all minds with the gutter garbage of humanity and the depraved debauchery of an immoral social order. This together with other compounding factors raised barriers to cooperation and the viability of faith-based communication to the present generation.

There was a time when faith-based scholars attempted to write commentaries explaining the dogma and then they began to translate scared writings into the language of the people. This was such a drastic change many of the translators were burned at the stake for their noble effort. The Old Testament was written in the Hebrew language, but the rabbinical system developed an oral Torah as a commentary. The New Testament was primarily written in *koine* Greek (*common supra-regional form)* and needed to be translated into other languages to be understood. The Islamic Holy Qur'an written over a 23-year period in *Classical Arabic* orally given to Muhammad assisted by Archangel Gabriel. Translation from the original language of the three Abrahamic faiths has been a major offense throughout history. This has perpetuated the freeze-frame thinking of most elements of human culture. Sadly, religion fell victim to the process.

This writer worked on a 42-year EVERGREEN Project to render *koine* Greek into a common devotional English instead of a classical Shakespearean (early modern) English. The purpose was to enhance the devotional value of the text in English the same way koine Greek was understood by a Greek-speaking population. One thing such a project teaches is when a unit of language is transliterated into another language, culture and time period, the original meaning may change. This is where academic excellence plays a role in such work. The objective of the EVERGREEN Project was to place words in the mother tongue speaker. This is why The EVERGREEN Devotional New Testament was called a rendering instead of a word-for-word translation to enhance the devotional value. What did the Greek word mean *"then"* and how can it best be rendered now in common English. For instance, the KJB translators chose to use the word "peculiar" from the Latin *peculium* meaning ones own property. It was a common word in 1611 but changed over time to mean strange or odd.

> *Who gave Himself for us, that He might ransom*
> *us from all wickedness, and purify a people as His*
> *personal treasure, eager for good deeds.*
> Titus 2:14 EDNT (Also, see 1 Peter 2:9)

Two things a reader of the New Testament should know: 1) The New Testament believers did not have a New Testament, only letters and parts which were read to them once and passed on to another group. 2)The Bible means "exactly and only what the first person who heard it read understood it to mean." How can an individual develop a relevant faith if difficult words and phrases from the past are not made clear? This is what ministers do in their weekly homily.

Chapter Ten

ASSERT
SUBSTANTIAL COMMONALITIES

Family life and education are primary in
constructive social change of a community.
Parents and teachers together supporting academic
achievement are the most essential elements of
teaching and learning. Teachers and learners must
have full support by adults in the home to enhance
subject matter sharing in the classroom. Homework
is where significant learning occurs; the classroom
excites and directs subject matter sharing through
assignments and evaluation of completed work.
Adults in the home are the "value added" boosters for
ambition and learning necessary for students to
become informed participants in the classroom.

All living systems have some sameness when compared; (Miller 2008) called this the sameness of the dichotomy. The more commonalities or sameness factors the stronger the comparison. Miller's Living Systems Theory (LST) may be applied to multiple disciplines to simplify complicated data. Consequently, LST may be used to better understand the sociology of the groups which make up a community. First, each level of a community: individuals (organisms), groups (made up of individuals), organizations (made up of groups), and communities (made up of organizations). Each level is made up of the previous one with individuals (organisms) being the common ground.

When data is gathered from individuals of a group or organization and compared one accrues valid and reliable data. It must be noted that individuals have different roles and functions (identity) in groups and organizations. When data is gathered by survey or interview from individuals, responses must be placed in categories:

> **Sidebar**: to secure reliable and valid information about a particular group, individuals from all areas of that group must have equal opportunity to respond to a survey or participate in an interview. This is done by sampling or using the total of the group. Data must come from the leadership, department heads, and various sub-groups.

In a church, for example: How did the staff answer, how did the deacons/elders answer, how did the choir respond? How about teens, senior members and new members? What about the response of a few visitors? When the data from each sub-group is determined and analyzed, the group may be understood as It relates to the specific survey or interview. All such research is a snapshot in time. Some areas of concern:

• business	• eldercare	• marketplace
• childcare	• family life	• police
• courts	• politics	• religion
• education	• healthcare	• service clubs

When animals, fish or fowls are compared within species they have some sameness. When all living things are compared, they have some sameness. It is a social research term used in methodology to create an artificial dichotomy by identifying a sufficient level of sameness to enable comparison.

The most overlooked aspects of common ground in a community is elementary and secondary education. Children, parents and teachers are stepping-stones to constructive community change. Parents as well as teachers have expected outcomes for students. All parents and particularly mothers have strong feelings and obviously wise and useful ideas about education. Positive social change is best begun with the children. To clearly understand what children, need, educators must listen to parents, especially mothers. It would be good for all educators to remember before public education and formal higher learning outside the home, mothers were preparing their sons to rule the world, lead armies, operate businesses, and be productive and wise citizens. Mothers may be the key to unlock the process of community change.

Adult involvement in the home is an essential aspect of academic achievement. My privilege was to be raised and encouraged by a teaching mother. A brain-storming event to give parents an opportunity to express their deepest desire with reference to their children's education produced a revealing and doable list of educational outcomes. My teaching career spanned four decades as a Graduate Professor of Education and Social Change and the sidebar below provides excellent expectations and learning outcomes. Perhaps most importantly: the hopeful outcomes came from parents of students.

Sidebar: *Analytical skills, writing and speaking skills, confidence in math, able to balance humanities and science; opportunity to test ideas in a safe environment, become problem solvers, become entrepreneurial, willing to step outside their comfort zone, learn to prioritize.*

Self-confidence and encourage others, willing to speak truth, resilience and adaptability, develop a moral compass, be patient and non-judgmental, be compassionate, learn peace maker skills, learn to win and lose, learn to face failure and overcome, learn the value of hard work.

Learn to survive disappointments, see beauty everywhere, experience joy, sadness, love, and peace and share feelings with others, set goals and be an achiever, develop a positive outlook, build relationship skills, *maintain good health habits, appreciate the value of life, liberty and justice for all.*

Follow their dreams and find their own path, know their strengths and weaknesses, develop self-advocacy and encourage others, become aware of the value of connecting with others. Plus, many unexpressed hopes and dreams!

In modern history, translations and new language renderings of past writings have become a common practice. However, one truth is often overlooked: when a document is translated and interpreted in another language or culture, the meaning and interpretation change. This is where culture, faith and language factor into social change. Those who desire to impact social change in a community must care enough to learn who the true leaders are, how they came to their present position, where the citizens originated, what baggage they brought with them, how their entrenched culture and religion could cause resistance to change and how the present circumstances came into being. Are most differences insignificant when compared with other groups? Are enough people known to initiate a conversation to find common ground? Can sufficient sameness be discovered to initiate a conversation?

Take for instance the 120 individuals gathered for prayer in the Upper Room at the Feast of Harvest were almost all from Galilee. Yet, the general public saw a common culture and asked, *"Are not all these -Galileans?"* They had developed a sameness as far as the public was concerned. There were some small differences but not sufficient to separate them into stranger groups. Should this not be the goal in social change and refuse to permit minor differences to hinder friendship or break fellowship when shared goals for change are beneficial to the community?

Friendship is the key to discovering the stepping-stones to common ground in a multicultural community. When individuals discover their friends have similarities and differences, the same way lovers are attracted to a significant other, their similarities prevail over differences. This may be an allusion, but it opens the door to friendship despite differences. What does this mean for constructive change in groups and communities?

Individuals change more easily that groups, but groups change faster than communities. The best place to start the process of social change is with friendly individuals. As differences are accepted, more similarities are discovered. When people learn to live with the allusion that people are different but that all humanity share many elements of sameness, the human race has a chance at survival and social progress can be beneficial to all concerned.

An understanding that a single person may impact a group sufficiently to alter attitudes and adjust goals is a significant step forward for social change. It is all a process which starts with individuals. When teen-agers become aware of common social ground and refuse to permit minor differences to hinder friendship, the process of change has begun. This facilitates maturity and cultivates connectedness and insures cooperation for social progress. Besides teenagers, the most useful group for positive change are parents because of their aspirations for their children. Parents are looking toward the future and are willing to cooperate with constructive changes that benefit their family and enable their children to have a better future.

All communities in a civil society would have some commonalities which must be considered by any group desiring to produce constructive change. A secular society would have certain observable characteristics of a mature social order which includes a resistance to change. Yet, history shows that when things stay the same, a stagnation and deterioration begin and develops a slippery slope to a moral and unsafe place to live. On the other hand, those with sufficient resources and a continuous income stream may isolate and insulate themselves in an upper-class gated community and become a gathering of elite and exclusive social slobs. The purpose of this book is not to assist an upper-class community that wishes to be left alone, but to assist the poor who need a save place to live and grow a family. The wealthy can stay behind their fences and gates which communicates, *"We are happy as we are and do not want any uninvited visitors."*

Some Community Commonalities

1. It may hold a worldview different from the faith-based values of Judaism, Christianity or Islam.

2. It may embrace a dominant culture that eliminates all aspects the sovereign rule of God.

3. It has learned to exist within its own diversity.

4. It is tolerant of inconsequential differences but opposes change which breeds intolerance and weakens the dominant culture or makes a difference in private and public life.

5. It will permit various groups to erode the dominant culture which will create pockets of resistance to the common good and work only for selfish change.

6. It seeks to solve problems with an environmental framework where people of various backgrounds may work together to achieve common goals.

7. All of this must be understood by those who desire constructive change to benefit the whole community. Such change may come in parts, but others must see that each incremental change is of value to the whole community.

The faith-based background or lack of may become a stumbling block unless each person approaches the community with an open mind and a transparency that is viewed by the community as *"sincerity with the best interest of others."* Those with faith-based standards often disagree with some characteristics and behavior of the community and declare an adequate worldview must include a Creator God and that all human affairs are under the sovereign rule of the Creator. Such a change cannot be prematurely forced on a diverse community. In such cases a spiritual dimension must be added to the strategy.

Common ground must be found together with an understanding that faith-based differences relate to the heart, soul and the afterlife, while cultural and social differences relate to the mind, will and emotions concerning the present life. The "now" is more powerful than an experiential relationship with a Power beyond themselves. A secular society has accepted civil behavior (*communal, daily, habitual, ordinarily* human), while spiritual behavior is (*transcendent, mystical, religious.)* This dichotomy has little sameness.

The three monotheistic religions: Judaism, Christianity and Islam are based on Abrahamic Faith because they accept the One God Who revealed Himself to Abraham and all three developed within Middle Eastern culture but in different languages. They obviously have similarities: faith in One True God, Creator and Sustainer of the Universe, accept personal sacrifice as an act of worship, perform good works, practice habitual hospitality, seek peace and justice and acknowledge an afterlife in the Hands of a Loving and Just God.

Common ground in religion is obscured by culture and language. These common areas are contrasted with diverse beliefs about God, distinct forms of worship, and different views of the afterlife. These differences have not been altered over the centuries. It is better to start with elements of social change rather than attempting to change faith-based thinking. Although religion is part of culture it is a difficult part to change. Outsiders cannot change a religion, only changed individuals within the faith may alter their personal beliefs and change some of their behavior. Faith-based change will be individual decisions not a group action. It is true, however, that individuals may mature and make personal changes in their faith-based lives. The sidebar below speaks to the inflexibility and resistance to even small changes by leaders in traditional religions. Without positive social change which benefits the whole community there is little hope of altering any faith-based action.

> **Sidebar:** Early in life as a Certified Public Relations Consultant, my work was with organizations and corporations with similar products and a common customer base. It was called AID, Ltd. [Associated Institutional Development, Limited). Working seven (7) years on a project to bring two small denominations together and avoid overlapping expenses and duplicated services, a Proposal was finally presented jointly to a mixture of thirty (30) select leaders from the two groups. After a long presentation showing how the two groups could work together and save almost $10 million annually in outgo, the project failed because the top leader of one group asked, *Dr. Green, what would we call this joint group*? Sadly, this had not entered my mind...only that they could save $10 million a year in operational expense by avoiding duplicated services. My answer was unreasoned and suggested a common identity. One group was willing to work with the new identity, but the old Bishop from the other group responded, "We are not willing to take "Holiness" out of our name." This killed seven years of hard work, viewing audits and interviewing people and taught me a valuable lesson. **Don't mess with historical religious words dear to the heart and soul of faith-based groups.**

Kurt Lewin developed in the 1940s a three-phase organizational change theory: 1) recognizing the need for change; 2) moving incrementally toward the desired change, and 3) finally solidifying the new changes as standard behavior. Lewin saw organizations frozen in their traditional ways and suggested the first step was to "unfreeze', thaw, warm up or soften the hardness. This is a world of continuous change, but the constant change provides an opportunity to guide the process in a more constructive direction. Change will take the way of least resistance. To paraphrase, Lewin suggested to navigate the process, the hard shell must be softened. This can be done by removing ten percent of the opposition which would be the same as placing ten times the positive force toward basic constructive change objectives. John Kotter developed a multi-step process for guiding change. It has been called "**THE BIG opportunity.**" Note the underlined words.

- ▶ **GENERATE** a sense of <u>urgency</u>
- ▶ **SHAPE** a course-plotting <u>coalition</u>
- ▶ **FORMULATE** a strategic <u>vision and initiatives</u>
- ▶ **ENLIST** a brainstorming group for<u> ideas</u>
- ▶ **FACILITATE** action by removing <u>barriers</u>
- ▶ **ANNOUNCE** short-term<u> wins</u>
- ▶ **MAINTAIN** <u>incremental</u> changes
- ▶ **SOLIDIFY** <u>constructive change</u>

The monotheistic religions believe God is eternal, omnipotent, omniscient, omni-benevolent and omnipresent. (known as *Yahweh* in Hebrew and *Allah* in Arabic). Christianity's perspective is a triangle view of God who is both transcendent and personal. From Creation to the birth of Jesus, the triangle rested on the Father; at the birth of Jesus until His Ascension, the triangle rested on the Son, and from the Feast of

Harvest (Pentecost) until the present age, the triangle rests on the Holy Spirit. This chronological perspective of God dealing with the human race from Creation to the historical present and beyond presents One God in three Persons: Father, Son, and Holy Spirit. This is similar to the multiple roles of humans as parent, child, and sibling with a connectedness to all others in the human race.

The culture of America is of Western origin, but has been greatly influenced by a pluralistic philosophy, character, moral standard and principles which include Africa, Native American, Asia, Pacific Island, and Latin America cultures. Almost every language of the modern world is spoken in the USA. Most frequently spoken non-English languages are Spanish, Chinese, French and German. Ninety percent of the population speaks and understands some English and most official business is conducted in English. Over time other languages are gaining ground on English.

English is a young language compared with others. It is a West Germanic language influenced by Anglo-Frisian dialects brought to Britain in the 5th to 7th centuries AD by Anglo-Saxon migrants from Northwest Germany, Southern Denmark and the Netherlands. This developed middle and modern English. Older languages greatly influenced English and other more modern languages. The various cultures of the world were deeply influenced by the language in which they developed. Note the sidebar on older languages:

> **Sidebar:** Tamil may be older than Sanskrit and is spoken in India, Sri Lanka, Singapore and Malaysia. However, Sanskrit may be the world's oldest language. All European languages were inspired by Sanskrit. It was spoken at least 5,000 years before Christ. Sanskrit

remains the official language of India; however, it is now used in worship and not spoken by the people.

Latin may be the third oldest and was the official language of the Roman Empire and Roman religion. Latin is in the romance branch of Indo-European family and is official in the Roman Catholic Church, the Vatican and considered a classical language and the basis for French, Italian, Spanish, Romanian, Portuguese and the most popular language when English was originated. Latin was the international language of most of Europe in medieval and premodern times. Books of all religions, higher literature, philosophy and mathematics were written in Latin. Hebrew and Arabic are both in the Semitic language family.

Chapter Eleven

ALLOW
INCONSEQUENTIAL
DIFFERENCES

Inconsequential differences should be acknowledged and accepted to the extent that they are not a deal breaker. An issue of difference that does not create an obvious division or cause a break in fellowship should be allowed without prejudice. Even identical twins have small variances that only the close family recognize. In spite of small ways twins are not the same, they are still called identical which means "similar in every detail or appear to be alike."

The two most distinguishable differences in culture are language and religion. The dialect of a mother tongue and faith-based behavior will appear different to the public. In fact, the traditional language and religion are foundational to the common life of an indigenous group. Most of the languages spoken today have roots in other language groups. The distinctive nature of language is much different than religion. Language has deeper and wider roots and languages are similar to others in many ways. They come for language groups just as Judaism, Christianity and Islam, three monotheistic religions were based on Abrahamic One God Faith.

Arabic alone has influenced over 12 million words in other languages. Any attempt to deny the use of an original language or traditional worship will cause feelings of great loss. However, a common language is basic to communication and social change. Many aspects of religion are intimate and private, such as, prayer and worship. Language is in the public domain with 24/7 day to day interaction. One may change their thoughts and feelings and even faith-based aspects of personal life without disassociating with friends. Altering one's language separates those who will not or cannot learn a new language. As people grow with a second language, they increase the use by associating with others who speak the same way. This causes some friends to be left behind.

Language has more commonalities and connections because of the nature and background of words. While religion and faith-based practices are precise and distinct in their association with a particular religion. Even in Protestant groups a minister can be identified by the use of certain language to a specific denomination. It is obvious in the three monotheistic faiths: Judaism, Christianity and Islam. Each have particular words, symbols, types of buildings, special clothing, eating habits, speech and language use that easily identifies them with their faith. In reality, there are both common areas and totally distinct aspects of each faith. This is part of the difficulty of changes in language and faith.

It appears that major religions want the world to follow them while they are not willing to seek or develop any knowledge or understanding of the particularities of both why and how the particular faith-based system works. Language has a daily marketplace necessity to function in the public square. This is not true of religion because it does not have to be exercised or practiced to function in the marketplace of the community where they live, work and worship.

The dominant group usually wants others to learn their language while refusing to study the language of others. A dominant culture does not adequately consider the value of reaching people in their mother tongue. Notwithstanding, the confusion of languages at the Tower of Babel which hindered a combined effort for a common task, the Jewish Festival of Harvest was an obvious example that God accepts various languages. Yet, constructive change is hindered without a common means of communication. When words are not clearly understood, hostility develops because one group is made to feel inferior or intimidated. Language is the first step in reaching any group. When everyone fully understands the purpose of social change, the other elements of culture become easier to handle.

The most difficult areas to facilitate change are religion and language. This is a big part of social change. Most faith-based groups use archaic terms or theological concepts to speak of their faith. There is a huge difference in the process of social change vs spiritual change. Humans can stimulate the need and process of constructive social change, but spiritual change requires an innermost and intuitive perceptional change which among other things requires the Hand of God. Social change advocates must walk softly and speak tenderly about the faith of others. Understanding people and their place in the world and their faith-based behavior requires assistance from a Higher Power. A sociologist, peace maker or a social worker does not possess the knowledge or power to alter one's faith; it is above their pay grade. Little attention is paid to clothing, food and family life, but interfering with one's faith-based thinking is often a deal breaker.

(Consider your own feelings should others question your religion when your parents and grandparents and friends all practice the same faith.)

Throughout history people living in proximity to those who speak a different language normally learn enough to transact business and establish friendly relationships. Any change in faith-based worship must come from within based on new information and fresh experience. In the history of sacred writings, individuals or groups were not required to cross cultural or language barriers to receive divine assistance. If it took an "unnaturally acquired" ability to communicate, there was a divine intervention. English as a common language of early America was readily adapted by early immigrants, but it took years for faith-based behavior to change and most never did. The language changed but the faith-based behavior was super glued to the heart and soul.

This brings the discussion to the history of language and faith-based communication. It appears that each national, tribal, or cultural group produced faith-based information in their mother tongue or a common language. The record of God dealing with the Hebrew nation was in the Hebrew language. Sacred writings for the Greco-Roman world were in Greek. Islam's faith was expressed in Arabic. Also, it seems that each major religion of the world was documented in the language of its founders or geographic origin often to the bewilderment of the rest of the world.

> **Sidebar**: In working with a doctoral student* from the Republic of China (Taiwan) to determine a dissertation direction, she was concerned that Chinese College Students resisted Christianity because they did not want to change their culture. She knew pictorial writing and was asked to write a few words: *redemption, wife*, etc. Then she was asked to explain the pictorial writing: *"redemption is a man under a lamb"* and woman is *"a man who works like a horse."* We looked at several more examples and finally she grasped that the concept of redemption and other theological concepts were buried deep in the culture of the Chinese language and that the Lamb of God that brought redemption was part of Chinese culture.
>
> ———
>
> *Chen, Lydia A. (1996) "Christianity and Traditional Chinese Culture" University Microfilm, Inc.

World history reminds humanity of wars and religious persecution over faith-based thinking in a different language. One of Hitler's expressed desire in initiating aggressive land grabs was to unite the German speaking people that had been scattered and were losing their common culture. This may have been an opportunistic excuse, but it worked for his place in history. Perhaps my mother's definition for excuse would clarify the issue, *"An excuse is the skin off a reason stuffed with a big lie."*

In modern history translations and new language renderings of past writings have been a common practice. However, one truth often overlooked is when a document is translated and interpreted in another language and culture the meaning and understanding changes. Thus culture, language and the normal way of life of a people are altered by the displacement of war, regional famine, migration, economic depression, persecution and social change. The negative causes of such human resettlement do not always have a positive outcome.

Forced migration instigates feelings of being stuck in a different place with no future and becomes grounds for people to congregate with groups of common culture and language with a hostile attitude toward their surroundings. They develop a ghetto mindset and become isolated with a feeling of inferior status with few and limited opportunities. The situation has a kind of sameness feeling. Most cannot go back to where they were or go forward to a better place. It would be helpful if instigators of forced migration would remember the Golden Rule *"Do unto others as you would have them do unto you."* Some statement relative to this rule may be found in most cultures clearly expressed in their language.

Social change is a task of the heart and soul and must be done slowly and with proper consideration for the feelings of others. The end is worth the journey provided it is approached with the proper attitude. The objective is constructive improvement for all the people by building a new community environment and facilitating agreeable interaction patiently considering the multicultural make up of communities populated by immigrants attempting to find a safe place for their family.

Positive social change requires the acceptance of small insignificant differences that relate to culture. All constructive social change must be in voluntary in small increments over time. There must be common consent and the process cannot be rushed. From a faith-based perspective, all the elements of various cultures cannot be accepted. All immorality, abuse, unfairness, insecurity, and behavior not founded in a respectful and well-mannered society must be carefully and prayerfully assessed directly with those who have authority to influence any changes.

A cultural framework for belief has created a brand identity for religion based on distinctive teachings. There is little effort to accentuate the common ground that exists for many faith-based groups. Judaism, Christianity and Islam all worship the One True God, Creator and Sustainer of the Universe: this is common ground, but specific ancestorial heritage often complicates interaction with other religions. Some worship multiple powers and this becomes a difficulty in positive social change. However, many individual's visible faith-based behavior is only culturally tied to the past and not truly spiritual devotion to the Supreme Power. It appears that many churchgoers on one day demonstrate this by their behavior the rest of the week.

Such behavior heightens the impact of differences rather than the commonalties. When the emphasis is on the *manner, tradition, place or time* of worship rather than on daily lifestyle, the difference divides the message into so many parts the public cannot construct the whole. Much of the meaning is lost in the diverse and segmented message. Only through commonalties may knowledge be advanced, yet faith-based congregations constantly emphasize their differences. This dissimilarity is a tragic flaw that divides faith-based groups where there should be a common agenda to make moral citizens of the community into naturalized citizen of heaven.

The whole issue of brand names for faith-based groups is confusing. So many different Baptist churches: American, Southern, Independent, Free Will, Conservative, Primitive, Missionary, Regular, General Baptists and the list continues. Other groups have various qualifying names as well. There is the Presbyterian Church (USA), Presbyterian Church of America, Cumberland Presbyterian, etc. Also, there are United Methodists, Wesleyan Methodist, Evangelical Methodist, Free-Methodist. The Restoration Movement did not intend to start a specific denomination but ended up with the Christian Church, Church of Christ, Disciples of Christ, plus independent Christian churches. How can the public make any sense of this stew pot? Then there are national groups, but all faith-based groups have either a language, cultural, ethnic or regional identity. These differences divide and hinder fellowship and constructive change. The multiple standards of behavior also bewilder the general public.

There are sound reasons for the names given to faith-based groups, but many add to the bewilderment of the public. The confusing names add more heat to the simmering stew pot. There seems to be no limit to the length some will go to create an uncommon identity. Then some groups have the same name but hold different tenants of faith. Although there are honest reasons behind the choice of names, the lack of commonality baffles the public. Just how does this fit into the concept of One Lord, One Faith, and One Baptism?

Confusion exists among faith-based groups as to the differences between being distinct and being distinctive. Part of the problem is a lack of understanding of the idea of being distinct. To be distinct is to be dissimilar and clearly seen. On the other hand, to be distinctive is to be one not commonly found elsewhere and suggests exclusivity. The attempt to distinguish one faith-based group from another on distinctively different teachings does not adequately present the group to the public. In fact, it breaks down the quality of the whole group by an emphasis on the lack of a unified message. Emphasizing the differences to distinguish one group from another is to distort the general impression of the faith-based movement. The public has a right to assume that a religious group would have sameness and share similar teachings with other groups that claim to be a part of the same whole. No part may be removed or left out for the entity to be whole. When significant differences in the various groups are evident, the public begins to question the validity of the whole. This creates a public identity crisis for all aspects of faith-based thinking.

The concept of identity is one of having sameness; however, differences exist within the individuals or groups that make up the whole. Even identical twins that develop from a single egg and are the same sexes have differences. Scholars do not note identical twins for almost indistinguishable differences, but for sameness. Their appearance is so similar that only close relatives can recognize the differences. It should be this way

within the faith-based movement. Those who are a part
of the inner circle may see the small differences and
understand their causes, but the public should never
have to sort through a jumbled story of cultural history.
A unified message of grace and faith should come from
the community who worship God. Since the differences
are not consequential enough to change the population
of heaven, they are not worth being a topic of discussion.
Individual interpretations of particular aspects of scripture
may exist, but a central theme and message should exist.
When sectarian views distort this common message, the
public is confused. Nor would it be fair and equitable for
one to force the way they prefer their steak cooked on the
rest of the world. Look at the dialects of language, the
difference in clothing, the variety of foods and music; it
would be impossible to put the whole world on the same
list of options.   Yet, this is what some religions wish to
do!

A family is a group that is similar and connected.
This association causes a blending of mind and heart.
Certainly, a family has differences, but the members
of the primary group are characterized by similarities.
One may speak of a family circle when describing close
relatives or a family tree when describing relationships.
The entity has a sameness that determines the
family identity.   Differences are normally put in the
background, as new members are welcomed into
the larger family circle. Whether it is the family photo
album or a genealogical chart, it is the sameness, the
similarity that identifies the kinship relationship. Have
faith-based groups lost the concept of family? Is there
no sameness? Must each group present a distinctive

message to the world and project a divided movement? The Family of God on earth deserves a simple and clear message to the world. What can be done when everyone wants their message to be the universal dictum rather than whom they worship?

There is room in most religions for cultural expressions of faith. The Godhead is presented in three personalities: Father, Son, and Spirit. Faith-based groups relate differently to each of the Persons in the Godhead. The Father is the Forgiver. The Son is the Savior, the Friend, the Assurance of one's relationship to God. The Holy Spirit is the Enabler, the Enlightener, a Guide to Truth, the Lawyer to plead one's case against evil, and the One Who Walks alongside believers enabling them to live and maintain a faith-based lifestyle in the midst of an evil and wicked generation. Likewise, family members relate differently to each member of the immediate family: father, mother, son, daughter, brother, sister and the near kinfolk. Yet, they are one family! Why can the faith-based groups not function as one sacred family under One God?

Each human being has different roles and functions. Yet, they are all part of one human race. One person may be a son, parent, sibling, spouse, cousin, nephew, a churchgoer, a ballplayer, a business owner, etc. with different identifying roles and functions, but a single human being and a multiple functioning member of the human race.

The fabric of families is made up of divergent strands which come together to form a single unit. It seems that two strands may be twisted together to form yarn for use in creating fabric, but at least three strands are required to braid or plait a strong and useful cord. Two strands alone cannot form a strong union; a third strand is required to provide strength for the unit. In the case of a couple coming together in marriage, this third strand is a sense of family that permeates the commitment and supplies the adhesive for a strong bond. The wise man Solomon said, *"Two are better than one and a cord with three strands is not quickly broken."* It is the third strand that Solomon considered the strength of the union.

The common message of faith and grace must be proclaimed by each part of the faith-based movement or the credibility of the whole is in jeopardy. The same is true of faith-based groups, when one group attempts to stand alone or limit association to a few who are "just the same," the binding strand which brings strength is missing.

There is some value in diversity, but there is vitality in common ground. Ancient writings were clear *"If the trumpet makes an uncertain sound who will prepare for battle?"* Groups that insist on projecting dissimilarity will remain weak without a sense of commitment to commonalties that could inform their participation in the larger community of faith.

Sectarian groups that isolate themselves from the whole by emphasizing the distinctive nature of a particular teaching rather than a common identity with the community of faith will suffer limitations and remain earthen vessels without the spiritual dynamic for faith-based advancement.

There is strength in unity and weakness in division. Sacred text was clear, *"If a house is divided against itself, that house cannot stand."* This was said in the context of the reality that Satan would never permit his work to be divided. Perhaps these differences within faith-based groups proceed from an evil strategy to "divide and conquer." Perhaps it could be that some individuals are attempting to build a kingdom for themselves or just gain personal wealth.

Such groups become "takers" without giving a fair share commitment to the infrastructure that forms the basis for their existence. Even groups that express certain uniqueness and differentiate themselves from others, receive nurture and sustenance from the larger community. Lacking a common identity with the community of faith, such groups do not contribute to the strength of the larger body. Any strand, which tethers them to the community of faith, becomes an umbilical cord carrying nourishment from the larger unit. This seems to be a one-way street. Scripture in Romans 11 explained a conceited and egotistical perspective, which resulted in *"taking without giving."* The character of an engrafted branch illustrated the idea. Paul said, "*You do not support the root, the root supports you."* (Romans 11:18)

A grafted branch does not support the root that nourishes its life, but the root supports the grafted branch. The grafted branch may live, grow and produce foliage and even fruit, but remains an unorthodox part of the larger unit. It often becomes mutant, militant and radical and is a liability to the original unit. The graft may also become a hindrance to growth and fruit bearing by sapping strength from the source.

An understanding of the concept of grafting may clarify the problem as it relates to faith–based groups.

One does not have to be a horticulturist to see the disadvantage of foliage without fruit or different kinds of fruit growing on the same tree.   Such a fact may be a novelty, but a hybrid has disadvantages. There is something artificial about a hybrid. A hybrid is produced in plants and animals through the mixing of two different species or varieties. It may be useful, but it is sterile. The mule is an animal hybrid produced by interbreeding a donkey and a female horse. It is considered to be stubborn and requires a great deal of patience to make it useable.

When faith-based groups are viewed as a whole, it may be seen as a mixture of diverse cultures or traditions, and possibly be classified as a hybrid by the uninformed. The public may consider anything multicultural in composition a mixture of good and bad. However, religion is more of a composite similar to a complicated piece of music of considerable size and complexity.   It takes years of training and practice to translate the music into the harmony intended by the composer. When it comes to the faith-based groups, the general population cannot hear the harmony in the complicated composition. Therefore, it behooves people of faith to work together to advance a common agenda and a sense of harmony. It is harmony which makes the melody pleasing and meaningful. It is harmony that relates to social change.

Perhaps the fig tree has a message. The fig tree was well known and common throughout scripture. They were useful.   Adam and Eve wore clothes made of fig leaves. Figs were used as a medicine for Hezekiah. The fruit bearing cycle of the fig tree was common knowledge.

The fruit grows on the fig tree before the leaves appear. Consequently, when Jesus was hungry and approached a fig tree in full foliage and found no fruit, He cursed the tree. Why did Jesus do this? A tree so full of leaves promised a good harvest of figs. The application is obvious. When a Christian group shows the signs of life and foliage, the public has the expectation that it will produce a harvest of fruit. When the group sends the wrong message to the public, the consequences are disastrous. The faith-based group that claims deep roots in pristine and historic Christianity, and does not produce the expected fruit, becomes an obstacle to advancing a Christian agenda.

There will always be differences, but variety does not have to be negative and create disharmony. A choir is made of different people singing different parts. This creates harmony. They are singing the same song in the same key and are brought together by the melody. Harmony is a joint exercise. There is a congruent arrangement of parts that interweave the different parts into a single whole. What happened to the hymns with common melodies that held the early congregations together?

A musical ensemble is a group constituting an organic whole and together produce a single effect. There is a careful and balanced integration of the whole performance with no place for a star performance. The presentation does not permit a single instrument or individual to stand out. The concept of a choir or an ensemble is the integration of all differences into a single harmony for presentation. The group presents the parts of a musical composition in harmonious togetherness.

Unison is the singing of parts in a musical passage at the same pitch and the harmonic combination of two tones an octave apart. This means that a musical scale having eight tones to the octave and using a fixed pattern of intervals can still produce harmony. With the existing variety in faith-based groups, a beautiful melody and harmony could be projected in unison provided each group could honestly subordinate their differences to a common spiritual grounding.

Early faith-based followers of the Way had "all things in common." They were able to gather together in one place in "one mind and one accord" as a family group. They sang psalms, hymns and spiritual songs, singing and making melody. Surely, they sang the same songs, in the same key, and made melody in their hearts. Melody comes from simultaneous musical notes in a chord and produces a pleasing sound. Why then do faith-based folk always use some chromatic half-step scale and make every slight difference stand out as if it were a solo part?

To be viable faith-based groups must make some spiritual melody and find true harmony in order to send an appropriate message to the public. Even with many voices there can be one message.   Discord and strife must be overcome. Contention and conflict must cease. Behavior and circumstances that mark the dissension must be controlled. A lack of harmony and the active quarreling among different groups has become a discordant sound that strikes the public ear harshly. Faith-based groups seem to fight the wrong battles. The conflict over creation and evolution is a good example of a battle lost when the deliberation gets to the courts.

Evolution was only a theory until a few well-intentioned zealots attempted to force beliefs which some held about scientific creation on the general public.   The consequence of the loss was that public education must buy textbooks that present evolution as fact rather than theory. Prior to the legal battle the textbook publishers were careful to present evolution as a theory not a validated fact. The lesson is clear: faith-based people often fights the wrong battle and become the loser.

The attempt to mandate morality through legislation during the days of prohibition in the United States did not work. Present laws are transparent about misguided efforts. Prostitutes are prosecuted while their clients go free. Criminals' rights are protected while the victims' rights and privacy suffer. The only hope is for common ground is build a faith-based bridge to society. Those who believe must penetrate society and integrate moral and ethical standards to the extent the law permits. In this process, principles must not be compromised.   To do this, differences must be put aside, and the areas of commonalties emphasized. Some of the present moral controversy exists over church and state, prayer in the schools, race, abortion, infallibility or inspiration of scripture, as well as the role of public or private education. Morality cannot be prescribed by the state or required by religion: it comes from within families and individuals. The issue of separation of church and state has been carelessly bantered about until the people have developed an inclination toward separation of God and State, a kind of secular society.

The issue of separation does not mean alienation. The issue has been blamed for a generation growing up without an adequate moral and ethical compass. Often problems of teen suicide, pregnancy and murder are blamed on the separation issue. This is more likely caused by a separation of God and state, because teen suicides, crime, and illegitimacy have been a blight on society for years. Some even claim these particular teen problems are a result of capitalism rather than secularism. Actually, the church and state split exist superficially as a concept much more than as a functional reality. Today many have banished the rich heritage of religious freedom. This requires denial of the inspiring history of forefathers who risked their lives and fortunes for freedom.

The state was not established to be free from religion; it just cannot take sides in the sectarian controversy that rages over cultural and religious issues. Faith-based groups that cannot agree among themselves are the best argument for the separation of church and state. Some do not understand that the government staying out of religion is the only security for individual freedom of in many areas of life. In a multicultural society the government cannot support a certain religion or endorse a specific faith group or embrace a sectarian position. What is the problem? The problem is simply that religious folk want the state to undergird their religion while they in turn neglect both the religion and the state. Some do not vote most do not participate in volunteer organizations; some do not exhibit high moral character or become spiritual and moral leaders. While religious groups argue about issues of little importance to society, the problems of society are left to the police, the courts, the foundations, and the para-church or non-profit issue groups.

Is the difficulty really prayer in the public schools? Perhaps the question should be about *"prayer in the home."* A faith-based experience should be sufficient to bring spiritual formation into the home. Parents should not abandon the teaching of prayer to the state or to individuals from a religion different from their own. The faith-based groups have not adequately taught parents the responsibility of preparing their children for participation in public life. During the early years, no one has more influence on children than parents do unless the responsibility is abandoned to the public-school teacher. Can the faith-based groups afford to provide one more excuse for parents to neglect their parental responsibility? A few more excuse "feathers" could break the back of organized religion and cause it to collapse inward upon the unsuspecting and uncommitted participants. The issue of race is also dividing both communities and faith-based groups. When good people differ on such crucial social issues, it points out the differences in the faith-based community. Jimmy Carter faced such a dilemma in his home area of Plains, Georgia. His difficulty was that politically and personally he could not abide segregation, but he did not wish to quit his lifetime habit of worship with a particular church. In his inaugural address as Governor of Georgia Jimmy Carter said, *"No poor, rural, weak or black person should ever have to bear the additional burden of being deprived of the opportunity of an education, a job, or simple justice."* He further declared that the time for racial discrimination was over. This was not true of his local church and this posed a great dilemma for this conscientious man. The pastor was dismissed over the issue. A new church was initiated because of the issue. For a time, Jimmy Carter tried to keep ties with his home church, but after his years in the White House, he began to worship with the other more tolerant church. Surely, the racial issue is more about culture than race; more about taught prejudices than honest human relationship, but racial and ethnic issues remain a problem in many faith-based groups. The issue still divides. Once divided, the next step is to be weakened, then to be conquered. Does a faith-based group have a future if it is not inclusive? Should grace not be shared with all who seek truth?

Can there ever be agreement on abortion? Can carnal individuals be persuaded to a moral position unfamiliar to the rest of their lives? This issue is an example of both the conflict of language and the conflict of moral and ethical philosophy. Everything immoral cannot be outlawed in a civil society; neither can one accept that everything that is legal is morally right. Both sides can easily set up a no win, either/or situation for the other side when the language and the culture does not permit such a distinction. The partial birth question has been a no-win issue for both sides of the abortion issue. The life or health of the mother, the issue of rape and incest create a middle ground that blurs the morality of the issue. Faith-based groups by dogma, tradition and pontificating on the issue created the no win situation. Reality for most people is clear on some aspects of the issue and blurred on others. Some suggests that only the mother could make the choice. Others say the state must control the issue. This is a no-win issue in politics. It is a controversial issue in faith-based groups. It is an ever-present social issue in each community and in most families. Yet the decision to let others decide weakens the core of common values and the moral and ethical standards of society. The same is true of many other issues on which both the church and the state take positions. This is one reason why faith-based groups do not work well in multicultural societies.

The battle over the Bible is basically one of an academic argument vs. a ministry argument. Since the original autographs of the scripture are not available for examination, it is academic to argue for infallibility of the original manuscript. This may be an excellent mental exercise for young academics studying for the clergy, but it has no place in the public discourse. When undereducated ministers or an honest layman attempts to deal with the concept of infallibility of scripture, they are over their heads. Truth cannot be affirmed without facts. Since no data exist, it is really a ministry argument based on the premise that the scripture is inspired and trustworthy for today. It is a matter of faith, not facts. Yet it is the ministry argument that becomes the basis for evangelism and missions. One does not attempt to explain the academic arguments used to support doctrine in these efforts. The trustworthiness of scripture and the love and concern of a personal God are the issues that count. When the faith-based groups abandon the ministry argument for an academic one it is simply preaching to the choir or the deacon bench; the general public is not listening.

Deep in the history of medicine is the concept of bleeding. It was a custom to cut and bleed individuals when they were sick to eliminate the bad blood. The barbershop was an early place for this practice. This is the reason for the red in the old barber pole outside the shop. Even the practice was used on President Lincoln after he was shot in the head. Could medical science have been so ignorant? The Old Testament clearly said, "The life of the flesh is in the blood." It is obvious the medical profession or the general public did not understand this adequately. It took many academic arguments in the medical community and much medical research to establish the true nature of blood as a source of life. Even medical procedures championed a few years ago have been abandoned for more productive interventions. Can the church afford not to be both practical and innovative in dealing with the basic moral and ethical character of humans and their interaction within society?

There is scriptural precedent for both the academic and the ministry argument. It is found in the two listings of the lineage of Jesus. One lineage traces the ancestry of Jesus back from Mary and another traces the ancestry back from Joseph. One related to the acceptance of Jesus as the Messiah for those who had not yet understood the concept of the virgin birth. The other lineage permits the academics to trace back from the mother that is the basis for the virgin birth doctrine. Medical knowledge did not exist at the time to explain that the blood of a fetus comes from the father. Later this was discovered, and the child was given the father's family name and the inheritance laws were established based on this fact. With this academic data, one can successfully argue for the Doctrine of the Virgin Birth. Yet it is an academic argument. That is the argument of Matthew, Jesus was King of the Jews. It is the argument of John that Jesus is Divine. Yet, Luke presents Jesus as a man and Mark presents the Savior as a servant. There is room for both the academic and the ministry arguments, but the general public today, just as in the days of Jesus, need the simple facts of the ministry argument: the written scripture is trustworthy as an inspired oracle of God to present Jesus to the world. Anything else is confusing and not productive.

Can abandoning the public school or putting Christian kids in church run elementary and secondary schools without adequate staff or curriculum reform education? Does the Protestant church have the funds to do this? Is the goal to establish a dual system of education: a secular humanist one operated by the state, and a religious one within the control of the church? If this is the objective, what about taxes, tithes, and tuition? Can the poor afford to pay taxes in support of the public school and tithes in support of the church ministries, then be charged tuition for "saving" their children from the secular humanists? Where does this leave the poor who hear the gospel willingly? Will they be abandoned to a godless system? Where is the battlefront in these matters? Perhaps it is in the home not the church

An overwhelming number of Americans believe religion is important in their lives. Research surveys verify that about 90 percent of Americans are religious and have some religious affiliation. Nearly 90 percent believe in a personal God who can answer prayer.

Some 84 percent of the polling sample believes that God still performs miracles. Tragically most of those who are religious do not participate in scheduled services presented by organized religious groups. Other recent research claimed that Americans were less likely to attend church but were not turning away from religion. In one poll 60 percent of the people claimed membership in a local religious institution, but only 42 percent actually attended services. Actually, membership has been on the decline since 1950. This decline has become a "negative participation" vote against the status quo, but little has changed. Local churches constantly seek new worshipers with little or no regard for those not present. If notice is taken of the absentee's negative participation it is often rationalized by something, such as, "They were not of us or they would not have departed from us." Obviously, most Americans prefer to maintain their faith in God, the Bible, prayer and even miracles without regular participation in scheduled services. If the general public has these beliefs, where does that leave the local church? Research data shows no effort in place that has checked the decline. Does this mean that the local church needs to find new and different ways of reaching out to build on the basic religious nature of the people? Should the church choose not to become relevant to the next generation, there would be little hope for an organized religious influence in America. The ability to influence society would once again fall to the effective witness of individual Christians.

More Catholics than Protestants believe that the human soul goes on to a higher level of existence after death, but nearly one fourth of those who consider themselves non-religious also hold that belief. More Protestants than Catholics presume that God performs miracles today. More Protestants than Catholics affirm faith in a personal God who can answer prayer. Although these findings are consistent with past research, they do not support any change in religious service participation. At first glance, it appears that the more education one has the less they believe, but that is not the case.

The problem seems to be an academic controversy versus a ministry argument. About 45 percent of individuals with a high school education or less believe the Bible is to be taken literally, word for word, compared to 15 percent with a graduate or professional degree. Some 21 percent of individuals with a graduate or professional degree believe the Bible is a book of fables, legends, history and moral precepts recorded by man. Only nine percent with a high school education or less hold this belief. This looks bad for the academic controversy over the literal interpretation of the Bible. Yet some 45 percent of individuals with a high school education consider the Bible to be the inspired word of God, compared with 64 percent of college graduates and 62 percent with a graduate2 or professional degree accept the ministry argument of inspiration of scripture. Contrary to popular understanding, the higher one goes in education the more likely they will consider the Holy Scripture used by the church to be inspired. This is an unexpected result from a survey taken by an international secular humanist magazine. It was taken because they were suspicious of past research by Gallup. They used the best scientific polling techniques. The results were surprising. Does this mean that the higher one goes in education the less one may believe the conservative church position of infallibility of scripture, or the more likely one is to believe in the trustworthiness of scripture as to inspiration? What does all this mean? Does it mean that the older more mature one becomes, the more attuned they are to the nature of the divine; consequently, they need an inspired text in which they can trust?

The church has never taken advantage of this aspect of higher education. Those with professional degrees are often more mature and deal daily with the mixing bowl of life. Could this account for their need to believe in the divine inspiration of the sacred writings? The professions are the teachers of the next generation. Public school personnel will spend more time with the young than either parents or preachers. The church should seek to utilize the older and the wiser as a means of reaching the next generation. The church must not abandon higher education to the secular humanist while the church concentrates on the elementary and secondary level as a primary effort to save the next generation. When more college graduates and individuals with graduate and professional degrees score higher than individuals with a high school education in accepting the Bible as the inspired word of God, one cannot blame the problems in the churches on education. It means that higher education has not been a problem of the church losing influence, but one of abandonment of higher education to a minority of secular humanists. Without a strong academic voice in the classroom of higher education, the church will continue to permit the secularists to influence the teachers of both today and tomorrow. The denominations, the local churches, and individual

Christians must accept responsibility for failure to reach the poor with the gospel and adequately influence higher education in the direction of faith. The basic faith is still there, the church has been unable to take advantage of the opportunity.

Too often the church has looked at the negatives instead of the positive aspects of higher education. The church should use the ministry argument of inspiration and advance Scripture as a tool to bring morality and ethics back into American society. The spiritual needs of those in higher education must not be abandoned to the secular state. The church has a continuing responsibility to higher education. While the Bible may be getting some respect in higher education, it is being neglected in the home. Research supports that the Bible has been reduced to an icon and has little practical use in the American home. Not only is the Bible neglected, most Americans lack biblical literacy. Many do not know basic facts from the Bible that they have heard all their lives. Almost 65 percent of Americans do not know that John 3:16 refers to a passage about believing in Jesus for eternal life. Many confuse old sayings with scripture and are unclear about most of the facts. A few thought the beatitudes were the wives of the disciples and that Joan of Arc was the wife of Noah. The excuse is a lack of time, difficulty in understanding Scripture and that it is not relevant to their daily lives. This speaks directly to the lack of relevance for the local church. The truth is that those who attend worship services regularly and listen to preachers almost every week are included among those without biblical literacy. Clyde Reid (1967) said the American pulpit was empty, because no one was listening. No one would have believed the matter could get worse, but it has. Many Protestant churches have lost touch with the people. No one is listening. Even those present find ways to avoid hearing the message.

The world is filled with sounds one never hears because of the limited auditory range of the human ear. Modern man is so assaulted by sound that many and sometimes most sounds are tuned out. Sound is a kind of fourth dimension. All sounds are witnesses of events taking place at the moment. Everything that moves makes a sound. Thus, sound before sight or touch tells one what is going on in one's personal space. Sound reveals complexities that vision alone normally misses. Hearing is an outgrowth of the sense of touch, the most personal of senses. Consequently, hearing is a personalized way of touching at a distance. As such, hearing is the most social of the senses and has particular meaning in the context of collective worship in a gathered church.

Some worshipers attuned to auditory evaluation possess the ability to enter a place of worship and through the sounds encountered assess the mood, pace and direction of the gathered congregation. This is both an asset and a liability to the local church.   Provided the worship is sincere and the spiritual leadership honestly communicating from the heart, the visitor and the regular congregants are moved to participate in the process of responding to the spiritual. However, in a congregation filled with strife, confusion, disagreement, a visitor and other participants can soon discern the nature of the gathering and extricate themselves quickly from the association. There is a story of a country preacher seeing a dog in the church isle asking a deacon to remove the animal. After the sermon someone told the minister that it was the Seeing Eye dog of a blind visitor. When the preacher apologized, the visitor said, "Oh, that's OK, that sermon wasn't fit for my dog to hear anyway!"

Scripture declared that the time would come when men would have ears to hear and hear not. That day has arrived. Even those who attend the worship service do not listen. They invent ways to block out the message, because to truly hear would require action. Three levels of "hearing" have been identified: 1) the level of non-hearing. The sound is heard, but not the words; 2) the level of hearing. The words are subconsciously recorded in the short-term memory, but the meaning and value are not considered. In such cases the mind, as a tape recorder, may play back the words just as they were received without an awareness of the meaning. 3) The level of listening. Here the individual receives the words, considers the meaning, and acts on the basis of the meaning to the individual. At the level of listening, one is compelled to respond and therefore act. When worshipers do not listen to the injunctions and challenges from the pulpit, there is little if any Christian action in society.

Politicians and clergy are weak surrogate proclaimers for the morality and ethical stands on social issues. Most Americans put both politicians and clergy at the lowest level of professional credibility. It is the people who should be speaking out about the issues that affect their lives and families. Even scripture warned that the "letter of the law kills, but the spirit of the law gives life." Unless America calls a cease-fire on the social and moral issues which plague society, the politicians or the clergy may never put their own houses in order. Without this truce there is little hope of finding workable solutions within a pluralistic society. A drastic difference in the ethnic and religious background of a multicultural society hinders the necessary networking of ideas and the webbing of human resources to find acceptable solutions to the sickness which plague a moral society. There is hope, but little probability of a cooperative effort in time to save the current situation. The big question is clear: can organized religion be restored to a worthy place in a civil society?   A corollary question begs an answer: can the governance of the people, by the people, and for the people be restored to the point that excesses can be eliminated, and the values of government be appreciated? Unless the faith-based groups reclaim their place of influence on the moral lives of society, the outcome of any constructive social change is doubtful.

Lack of agreement and conflict over basic central truths wounds the heart and soul of faith-based entities and sends an ineffective and impotent message to society. Institutions may not have the capacity to bring about the change necessary to produce a unified message, because individuals change more quickly than do institutions. Consequently, drastic change in the personal behavior of individuals is the best hope for renewal in faith-based groups. The emphasis needs to be on the personal behavior of individuals rather than group or institutional activity.

Chapter Twelve

AGREE
TO A SOCIAL CHANGE TIMETABLE

Social Change Timetable is slow. Everyone is in a hurry to make changes in the lives and circumstance of others. The constant effort seems to change the way others look, live, and love. Haste makes waste and reality must be faced squarely. It often takes as long to solve a social problem as it took to create the problem. The effort must be to make small incremental changes that are beneficial to most residents of the community.

Some gender, racial, ethnic, religious, language and national origin issues have been with sections of society for hundreds of years. This clearly means that change will be slow. Some are too eager to make changes in the lives and circumstances of others. Does this mean constructive change can never happen in in the near future? Probably, small changes may come in the "*not too distant future*" that is just after the *near future.* Of course, not! However, understanding the social change timetable does assist the appreciation for the small changes one sees and increases the tolerance for the gradual improvements that are taking place in society. Is the change moving fast enough? Of course, not! Social change must be paced, peaceful, and softly pitched: it is not a hard ball game, it is soft ball; in fact, it is *"slow pitched"* softball. Sometimes it is plaid without a ball; ideas and suggestions are *"soft pitched"* to the active people of the community to get feedback.

Communities clearly have a future, but a conclusive statement regarding this future in a multicultural society cannot be predicted without existing facts. There is too much controversial evidence, too many different opinions to make a conclusive proposal without more knowledge from the people living in the community. Outsiders do not know and must learn from the residents the good and the bad (and the ugly).

Constructive social change will not come by the might of a great speaker or some politically correct program, but by the spirit of renewal working though moral individuals who are committed to share what they in time, energy and resources. Positive humanitarian action and Personal transparent service which demonstrates a sincere interest in the people may be best way to start on the right foot. When people seen interest, sincerity, goodwill, and a little civility. they respond in kind. It may take marching around the walls several times before one can find a point of entry. This behavior can break down the barriers to progress and produce beneficial social change.

A "Together/Strong" group must be representative of the community and committed to constructive change for both family and faith and have courage of convictions with demonstrated spiritual humility. Progress in social and/or spiritual change always occurs in small increments over time. It cannot be rushed; there is a timetable attached to change. It is similar to the steps in growing a garden.

1. Diligent cultivation
2. Careful and Hopeful planting
3. Unceasing effort
4. Constant attention
5. Saintly patience
6. The law of diminishing returns
7. Must be touched by the Hand of God

In the past, there were hard times when families were urged to plant vegetable gardens to supplement their food supply. Growing a garden taught families that God was involved in the process, but there was plenty of work for the Gardener. I am reminded of my Grandfather's award-winning crop of corn. One Sunday a city slicker visited his church and was invited to lunch. After the meal grandfather proudly took the guest to see his award-winning crop. The visitor thought grandfather was too proud of his work and declared *"You should give God credit for this crop. He provided the soil, the minerals, the rain and sunshine."* Grandfather's response was simply, *"God sure left a lot for me and the boys to do!"*

Gardens were so prevalent during the war years in Great Britain that everyone still calls their backyard a garden. Now in better times they grow flowers, ground cover and shrubbery. The young and the poor have forgotten what grandparents and parents knew about gardening. Planting and growing a garden not only provide lessons for the young and the poor the value of growing a fresh crop; it makes them aware of divine intervention in their lives. A garden must be touched by the Hand of God regardless of the hard work of cultivating the land. Guidance in growing a garden also provides knowledge that plants are different and that they need to be organized and given special care. This knowledge may assist the poor and the unemployed through hard times; also, learning the lost art of growing a garden may become a life saver during future hard times.

Again, the process can be nudged a little, but it cannot be pushed beyond the norms of a social change timetable. Part of the problem is that minority groups have raised their expectations beyond the limits of normal social change. Change takes time. Time must be given for people to adjust. Higher levels of change would require a drastic revolution such as a civil uprising, a global pandemic or an economic or political   battle that spills over into the personal lives of local people. Tolerance must be taught; prejudice must be fought, and the spirit of progress must be caught before common ground develops firm enough for walking without boots. Discrimination must be condemned and punished. Honesty and fairness should be awarded. And all behavior should be influenced by a moral standard. Trust prevails in friendship and transparency solidifies relationships. Then, an only then, can a multicultural society live in peace and safety with the prospects of beneficial change.

Normally, a population will accept a *group of other people* into their community to the degree the group exists on the national scene. Since people gather in groups according to cultural orientation, food, clothing, music, language, religion, politics, and ethnicity, when a single group grows in a given community beyond the national norm, discrimination begins. This at first is a natural behavior until the prerogatives: who, what, why, how are adequate. Who are these people? Why are they here? From where did they come? There is a lessening of mistrust as an awareness of these answers develop, but as crime, loss of jobs, and negative personal encounters increase disapproving attitudes are expressed.

Resistance to *"the interlopers"* is quite at first, then it begins to take on a life of its own and grows until group violence beaks out. Laws, housings and school zoning, political redistricting, highway and street construction or any effort to fence in a minority cannot stop the growing feelings of resentment. Often it is the "late comers" who protest the most, forgetting their recent acceptance in the community. Surely, it would be better if everyone would accept the family across the street as part of the community, but it will not happen until moral clarity is increased, growth and peacefully and worship how, where and when they choose. Faith-based people have generally neglected to be fair and unbiased in such matters. Should the tables be turned such folk will feel the wrath of the community. Transparency and sincerity must be transparent in the lives of all who profess a high standard of morality and ethics.

In social theory, one learns that individuals change more rapidly than groups; groups faster than communities; communities easier than society. An affirmative attitude is needed to make a drastic difference, but legislation or groups of people are not the objective. Individuals are the persons who can change. Influence changes individuals and individuals change groups. Then, small groups can change the communities of which they are apart. Eventually, society will gradually feel the force of social change. When it is gradual over time, society is more apt to accept it. Rapid change has unpredictable consequences and may be feared the same way people become apprehensive about cancer or a global pandemic. Fear may turn into distress, anxiety may become dread, and alarm can spread panic. All change may become disconcerting unless people are fully informed or gain knowledge as a participant in the process.

Chapter Thirteen

AVOID
THE EXCLUSIVITY PARADIGM

Groups may be divided by social attitudes:
pluralistic, exclusivist, or inclusivist. Pluralistic
groups are a mixture of race and cultures and
limited in society. Exclusivist groups exclude others
and solicit a socially sophisticated membership.
Inclusivist groups are broad in orientation and scope
and appear to be openminded but are biased toward
those who do not accept their way. Others see this
group as an unregulated social club.

Many groups seek quantity rather than quality.
The desire to be the largest often weakens the effort
toward excellence. A faith-based entity should be both
adequate and effective. Quality and quantity are mutually
exclusive; increase one and decrease the other. There
must be proportional balance between these two
elements to maintain a viability in any organization. The
dynamic aspect of organizational growth goes through
predictable stages. A failure to understand these phases
freezes the thinking of a group into fixed attitudes that
handicap the effectiveness of any progressive endeavors.

All phases of growth are temporary; consequently, there is no continuous growth. This aspect of growth must be understood to avoid obstructions to development. The constant effort to push quantity neglects the quality needed to support and strengthen the basic operational structure.   The striving to construct the largest building or the effort of one local group to attempt all the services which should be shared with other like-minded friends is an impossible dream. This brings to mind the dreams of the builders of the Titanic.

The Titanic's builders wanted to build the largest ship on the ocean. This was a noble goal, but their *ego* was larger than the shipbuilding technology and material of that day. Why did the Titanic sink? It hit an iceberg--not really: it sank after striking an iceberg. The Titanic sank quickly because the quality of steel used was unable to withstand the extreme cold. The size of the ship also contributed to the breakup of the steel construction. It sank because the lookout in the crow's-nest was alert and signaled the bridge so the ship could turn in an effort to avoid the obstruction. The lookout was correct to warn the bridge. The crew was correct in turning sharply. Had the ship rammed head on into the iceberg it probably would have remained afloat or at least it would have taken longer to sink, and many passengers could have been saved. By sideswiping the iceberg, the hull was damaged, rivets popped, and the quality of steel was unable to withstand the cold and pressure.

The steel in the ship was brittle and could not absorb the massive amounts of pressure brought on by the water filled compartments.   The ship literally broke apart. The real problem was the high sulfur content of the steel from which the ship was constructed. This made the steel fracture in the cold water under pressure. The steel makers used the best technology available and thought they had done a good job. They did not understand the concept of brittle fracture caused by high sulfur content in the steel. In reality the shipbuilding design and technology was ahead of the knowledge of the steel makers. Those who made the steel were long dead before the technology was advanced sufficiently to explain the disaster.

The steel used in the Titanic was not declared the reason for the disaster until eight decades after the disaster. The largest ship of the day, designed to be unsinkable, sank within three hours of clashing with the iceberg. Some of the richest men in the world went down with the ship's captain and the architect who designed the unsinkable Titanic. The sinking of the ship made changes in shipbuilding, the procedures for handling lifeboats, and in maritime communication. Yet, it was several generations before shipbuilding steel advanced sufficiently to meet the dreams of the architect or the maritime company.

The moral of the Titanic tragedy is that dreams may not be enough. It is not sufficient to have a good idea; one must understand the unintended consequences of plans and actions. Even doing a job well is not sufficient to avert human disaster. The steel makers, the ship builders, or even the alertness of the lookout in the crow's nest or the quick and proper response of the crew on the bridge could not make the difference in the design or the faulty steel with which the architect's dream boat was constructed. It also suggested that the problems of life should be faced head on, and the consequences taken. Usually attempts to avert disaster fail because of previous faulty human reasoning.

Normally, everyone participating in a public-spirited or a faith-based entity honestly believe they are exclusively the right people with the better program to complete the faith-based or humanitarian task. However, there must be unity of purpose and agreement on the process for any endeavor to achieve the stated objective. Consensus is a key construct in planning and executing social or compassionate undertaking.

Abrahamic faiths are monotheistic, but Judaism, Christianity and Islam accept one God but have different paths to reach a positive afterlife. However, since there is but one God there should be unity among His People. An overriding need for all humanity is unity and cooperation in providing liberty and justice for all as they seek food, shelter, safety and salvation for themselves and their families. In an effort to make individuals moral citizens of the community and ultimately mystical citizens of heaven, there is a need for basic truth stripped of cultural complication of the divine path to the Promise Land. Some say, "truth judges, divides and separates" people so we must all "love one another and live and let live," yet, love without truth is a false positive or an error which causes the acceptance of an assumption. All roads do not lead to paradise. This is the major problem faced in community social change because it always includes variations of faith-based reasoning based on freeze-frame thinking and cultural complication mixed with ancestral traditions. How then do we proceed? In every situation God provides a way to plow around the stumps and concentrate on aspects of community disorder, discomfort, disease, and denial of the obvious simplicity of order. *God is not willing that any should perish, but that all should come to the knowledge of the truth.* When it comes to difficult human issues and problems of personal faith, perhaps this should be seen as God's work and not human endeavor alone.

The children need nutrition and education, teenagers need training for a vocation and life, families need guidance in childcare and problem-solving skills, and faith-based entities need a broader view of the world and a deeper under-standing of the ancestorial background which created their culture and traditions. For example, if one attempts to learn Spanish, they will hear a story about a King Ferdinand, who spoke with a lisp, and Spaniards imitated his pronouncing of z and c with a lisp. Whether this is true or not it is an explanation for the different way some speak in Spanish. My youngest sister, a Psychiatric Nurse, at age 83 still pronounces certain words the way her first teacher did. Some of the aspects of culture and faith-based behavior may have such a weak under-pinning. Those who plan and develop the structures and organizations for social organizations could learn from the Titanic disaster.   Size and money did not make a difference. Many of the plans from the past and the organizations built on the reputation and good name of previous leaders are simply accidents waiting to happen

Sidebar: research was done in Dallas, Texas at a large meeting of clergy where a new Moderator was to be elected. It was hypothesized that if a certain man were elected who dropped his right shoulder when he walked that some young ministers would imitate him. He was elected and within 30 minutes some young men were dropping a shoulder when they walked. It had nothing to do with faith but did show that some behavior was based on imitation of others. All ancestors, parents, teachers, leaders have individual aspects of their ideas and values that others will adapt their behavior to match those who appear to be successful. Truth and behavior are often "caught" rather than taught. "Monkey see... monkey do!"

The structures of the past do not adequately inform the present. Man was originally made in the likeness of God; however, it appears that when men make, develop or launch something it is in their own image. Their fingerprints are all over the operation and the basic benefits are for themselves. The mindset of the Tower of Babel still exists in aggressive human beings. They want to build the biggest, the best, the most-grand place on Mother earth, but it is man-made and has a limited viability and soon obscures the human labor.

Sidebar: a slave architect who supervised the building of a great pyramid tomb for an Egyptian King had a premonition that as time passed the blowing sand would wear away the King's name, so behind the official name he placed his own. Centuries passed and sand and weather wore away the King's name and revealed another. It was assumed to be the unknown slave architect who build the structure. Nature does at times give credit where it is due.

My father, Herbert Barton Green (1907--1937) had rheumatic fever as a child and was told he would not live out his teen years. By the grace of God and good doctors he lived to be thirty and fathered three children. He was a Deacon in Signal Mountain Church, and a manager of American Lava Corporation with an aggressive drive to live and leave his mark. He had a special way of carving his initials HBG on trees with one cut lines so as the tree grew his one cut line would open. Many years later his brothers showed me his initials on many trees. He has been gone for 84 years, but someone remembers and shares about his life with me. I was only 4 at his death. What is the lesson?

Nothing stays the same; everything changes. Even the Book of Genesis shares a simple message: human life began in a garden and the book ends, *"So Joseph died, being a hundred and ten years old: and the embalmed him, and he was put in a coffin in Egypt."* (Genesis 50:26) The lesson was clear: from a garden to a coffin and what counts is what happens between. All things man-made are limited by natural forces. Regardless of the ethical and moral nature of the enterprise, the human factor is still a liability. Consequently, it is evident that the primary concern during our short life should be the afterlife.

If a community is to be changed for the better, good people must maintain a friendly presence. Some called this stage of social change as a ministry of presence. A determined effort to associate freely within the community must be an ongoing endeavor. Those desiring to influence social change must engage the people in friendly conversation on their home turf. To complete the process of relationship building, one must create a relationship where the outsider is seen as a good and honorable person who has the best interest of others at heart.

The early contacts must not be seen as interlopers working for political advantage, or faith-based do-gooder attempting some charity work. The targeted individuals must see themselves as the beneficiary of something good and valuable to create the atmosphere conducive to friendly exchange of ideas. Friendship may not be the best place to start; in fact, friendship must be earned over time. One cannot listen without clothes, shoes, food, or a place to sleep. Once a positive presence is established, the normal steps can be taken to make a difference in the community through positive relationship building.

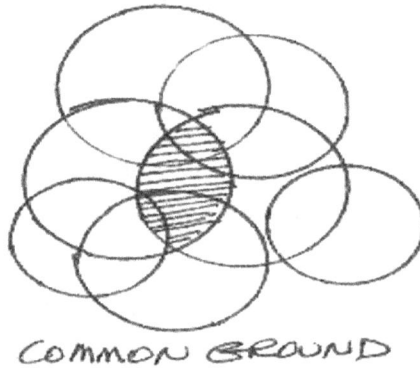

COMMON GROUND

Cultural Overlap Creates Common Ground

Chapter Fourteen

ACCULTURATE
FAITH-BASED BEHAVIOR

Never neglect the experience which produced the wisdom of the elderly. During their trips around the sun they witnessed God's Lighted pathway. Daily they have learned the best way up the Hill of Difficulty and through the valley of despair. They learned from hardships and yearn for a better life for their children. They can teach us these lessons. We should listen!

Acculturation is when an individual, group or population adapts or borrows traits from another culture. As contact is prolonged, an emerging of cultures occurs. The first place to notice acculturation is among the children who have not yet been taught prejudice and hate for those who differ. Early in life individuals have a capacity to see beyond the peculiarities of dress and behavior to the character of an individual. Children, dogs and the elderly appear to have a sixth sense in recognizing the good in people while adults seem to discriminate on the basis of difference and accept only others on the basis of similarities.

Provided most faith-based people looked closely at the dedication and devotional lifestyle of followers of other religions, they would find something to emulate and acculturate into their own lifestyle. Traveling in over 100 countries pursuing humanitarian and missional endeavors, many behaviors were witnessed which caused me to rethink my devotional life. Some observers minimize such an observance and pass it off as culture or traditions. My response to this perspective is clear: "Christianity has a culture and sacred traditions that are neglected or abused by some who claim to be faithful." This book does not have sufficient remaining pages go list all such failure to live the missional lifestyle proposed by Jesus, *"As you personally go into all the world, make disciples...."*

One classic example is the lifestyle of prayer. **Muhammad Anwar El-Sadat, President of Egypt**, who was assassinated by extremist army **officers opposed to his signing a peace treaty with Israel.** Watching extensive news about Sadat's dedication to peace and stopping a 30-year war, the **hard skin *callus*** *was obvious on his forehead. It showed his faith-based commitment to regular prayer on his knees with his forehead on the prayer rug. When his callus and commitments were compared to my personal prayer life, it was a wakeup call. President Sadat was a dedicated man to his faith-based practices.* **Most would improve their spiritual life by adapting some traits from Sadat's faith-based culture and commitment to daily prayers and consistent worship.**

Sadat and Begin

I was significantly challenged when Sadat placed his hard skin callused forehead against Begin. It appeared that he was implying *"I have been praying for you!"* How many faith-based people neglect this sacred exhortation? Islam requires adherents to pay five times a day kneeling with forehead touching a prayer rug. The friction creates the "**prayer bump**" and Islam society recognizing it as a "**devout sign**."

> *I exhort first of all, that petitions, prayers, intercessions, and thanksgivings, be made for all mankind; 2. for kings and all who hold high Responsibilities, that we may lead a quiet and tranquil life with reverence and dignity. 3. It is good and to do this is pleasing in the sight of God our Savior; 4. who desires all men to be saved and come to the knowledge of the truth.* 1Timothy 2:1-4

Multiculturalism is confused with cultural pluralism because of many similarities. Pluralism has a dominant culture and multiculturalism does not. Pluralism normally weakens the dominant culture without intentional effort and easily alters the society into a multicultural entity. When a society has an assortment of beliefs, cultures, ethnicities, backgrounds and traditions, it is pluralistic However, a multicultural community also has people of various nationalities, languages, religions and cultures living together, but has no cohesive, consistent or central culture. There are different cultures, various traditions, uncommon lifestyles, mixed moral values and behavior based on situational ethics which are celebrated and shared. This is the challenge faced when faith-based groups are plotting a course for presenting the substance of their message in a multicultural community.

To accept the structures of the past as sufficient for the present and the future is a false positive. This is certainly not true in any other aspect of the history of society. Local faith-based gatherings consist of people, and people change. Groups of culturally based religious people exist in a society, and societies change. Change is the one constant factor of modern life. The structure, message and substance of the faith-based message must change to maintain any semblance of viability for the present and future generations.

For example, the Jewish and Roman cultures began to overlap before the Christian Era and the early believers navigated a narrow pathway through the dominate Roman cultural maze and became known as "*the way*" and established a common integrated sub-culture. As individuals and families attached themselves to their teachings, their sub-culture spread and began the righting process of an upside-down world by making disciples, teaching all that Jesus began to do and teach. Water baptism was a spiritual initiation to identify converts with this teaching and learning process.

Early converts who grew in grace became known as disciples and gathered in houses as places of worship when Greco-Roman culture and religion were dominate in the known world. This culture worshipped multiple gods and goddesses and paid homage to a man who claimed to be a god known as Caesar, while those who followed *the way* worshiped a God who became man and was called Jesus. When the Roman state required citizens and subjects to be devoted and participate in public idolization of their gods as a duty to the state, those who chose not to follow or respect these strict requirements were persecuted or fed to the lions.

Those of *"the way"* encountered homogeneous groups as they traveled: Jewish folk were in a synagogue, followers of Jesus gathered in homes for daily worship, teaching, breaking of bread and the fellowship of believers who shared the same belief and behavior. The unconverted did not normally gather with believers; they were encountered in the marketplace, the fields or the roadside. When their life-direction changed, they began walking on "*the way*" and joined in the fellowship of the separated ones. Those who did not accept the new sub-culture openly opposed the disciples and their converts.

> *4. And some believed and spent time in the company of Paul and Silas; many God-fearing Greeks and influential women also believed. 5. But the unbelieving Jews moved with open resentment and recruited a mob of wicked and vicious men from the marketplace, and threw the city into confusion, and besieged the house of Jason intending to bring Paul and Silas out to the people. 6. When Paul and Silas were not there, the mob took Jason and some brethren to the officials of the city, accusing them,* **those who upset the whole world have come here also;***7. and Jason received them: and all these do contrary to the decrees of Caesar, saying that there is another king, One Jesus. 8. Hearing the accusations troubled the mob and the officials of the city. 9. And when Jason and the others posted bail, they were released.* (Acts 17:4-9 EDNT)

The progressive decline of faith-based gatherings is not inevitable. The worship of God has survived in many cultures; it depends on the commitment of leaders and members to a faith-based system. In a pluralistic or a multicultural community some groups are able to expand their sphere of influence, but immorality, opposition, persecution and weak leadership often cause decline. After Saul of Tarsus was converted, he explained his previous life in the Jews' religion, *"how with fanatical zeal he persecuted the new way and tried to destroy it."* (Galatians 1:13 EDNT): the KJV used *"wasted"* to translate the Greek word meaning *the opposite of building up.*

Tragically, in the present-day local congregations seem to be fragmented, stagnant, and unable to convey a unified message of grace to their constituency or the general public. There is no faith or behavior common denominator, no singleness of mind, no unity of purpose and little or no sharing of faith-based principles Differences constantly divide leaving little common glue to bind things together. Surely there is a path to common ground in faith without sectarian and partisan ideas and values. What is that common grounding? It is a faith-based lifestyle grounded in the worship of a Heavenly but personal God.

Jesus never asked His followers what they believed; He only asked, *"Who am I?"* (Mark 8:27-29) The common grounding is in "all *that Jesus began to do and teach"* to His early followers. This is what the only Gentile writer of the New Testament wrote to the Roman citizen Theophilus. (Acts 1:1-11). The contrast is clear in Luke's two volumes. Luke presented Jesus as God who

became man to a Roman audience who worshiped a
man who claimed to be a god. The Romans called their
man/god Caesar; Luke made it clear that he worshipped
a God who became man, and His Name was Jesus!
Luke overwhelmingly used "Jesus" instead of "Christ"
permitting others to use the Messiah reference.

In an early and emergent form, the fundamental
elements of pristine faith were presented in Luke's writing
to Theophilus. The gospel was written to provide clear
and often repeating basic truths. From the study of eye-
witness accounts, Luke was convinced that the past
details had present value. From these witnesses, Luke
gathered basic constructs from which he formulated
some first principles to guide the early Gentile believers
along their journey to a mature and growing faith.

Many original facts have been overlooked or
neglected by present faith-based leaders. This work is
an effort to draw fresh attention to historical facts which
still speak truth to power for believers today. Even though
Luke demonstrated great academic skill in presenting the
Gospel record and the early history of spiritual leadership
in the Acts of The Apostles, the "inspiration" of Luke's
work has not been challenged by historical records or
serious academics.

Aware of emphasis by position and proportion,
it is good to note that Luke's Gospel and the Acts
cover about one-fourth of the New Testament, about
the same proportion as Paul's writings. Luke's ethnic
and professional background provides an academic
excellence in Greek not seen in much of early sacred
writings, but Luke 1:1-4 describes his research skills
and he presented significant details others omitted.

Since Luke was a Gentile physician, he was concerned with Jesus' ability to heal; consequently, Luke wrote that Jesus *"healed all that had need of healing."* (Luke 9:11 EDNT) It seems that healing was reserved for those who needed to be healed so they could follow Jesus. It was part of the process of enabling individuals to become both a learner and a follower of His guidance

Luke intended to write a book that would convince those in the Greco-Roman pagan culture that the claims of Jesus were valid. He addressed the gospel story to the most excellent Theophilus, a title normally left for a high Roman official class. Luke's Gospel was to the Gentiles, presented in a universal manner with no concern for the Hebrew culture. He dealt with prayer, women, praise and historical facts in a manner unlike other writers of scripture and he used the best Greek in the New Testament.

Some are not aware that upper class Romans were also taught Greek. And that Jews in the Roman Empire hired Greek Slaves to teach their children Greek.

Whether a bond-slave or a servant, neither has full knowledge of what their Master does. However, there is a place of intimacy with God where His followers know what HE is doing in their lives. This state is called "FRIENDS." This is a good place to be!

15. I no longer call you bond-slaves; because a bond-slave does not know what his lord doeth: **but you I have called friends; for all things that I have heard of my Father I have made known to you.** *16. You have not chosen me, but I have chosen you, and appointed you to go out and bring in fruit, and that your fruit should remain: and that you should obtain answers to your prayers to make them fruitful.* (John 15:15-16 EDNT)

All things made by man's design are limited by the human element. Regardless of the spiritual nature of the enterprise, the human factor is still a liability. Consequently, it is evident that the primary concern during our short life should be the afterlife.

Troubled days follow human birth
As a suckling reaches Mother earth.
A stumbling earthling emerges to life
Bursting forth with a budding delight.
Walking with a stumbling gait
Trouble lurks at the garden gate.
Youth blossoms in the morning light
Withering age is reaped before night.
The frailty of life takes a final nod
Reaching for the hand of a loving God.

(Job 14:1-2 EDOT))

Chapter Fifteen

APPEND
LIFESTYLE TO AFTERLIFE
MESSAGE

*Assisting social change through missional behavior
is part of God's Plan. When God started the first
human family, He furnished a lush garden,
appropriate shelter and plenty of fruit and vegetable,
water and flowers. To do God's work is to assist with
affordable housing, food, safety, family and friends
in a livable community with happy children*

**Many individuals consider an afterlife from
a positive perspective presuming on the mercy
of a loving God.** This happens without any personal
responsibility to live a moral lifestyle as preparation
for God's provision. There is no willingness to trade a
present moral lifestyle for a future mansion in Glory Land.
Even some who heard the true message of grace were
not willing to weave a moral lifestyle into the fabric of
their faith with reference to the afterlife. To be worthy
of becoming a mystical citizen of heaven, one must
become a moral citizen of the human race. Most faith-
based teachers emphasize the afterlife without adequate
guidance about a moral lifestyle as a prerequisite. A

great price was paid for human redemption and loving hands have prepared a place for believers who accept God's grace. Why would anyone think a moral lifestyle would not be a fair down payment on a divinely built place in God's paradise?

Missional living is working together with God and others to bring constructive change and the message of love and grace to all who will listen. Wisdom brings authenticity and genuineness to the daily lives of those willing to be an active witness and faithful witness. **A faith-based lifestyle includes *missional living outside your comfort zone and adopting the attitude, thinking, behaviors, and practices of a missionary in order to assist others in becoming a moral citizen of society and a mystical citizen of heaven*.** *This is a progressive process to change individuals, families, and communities of advancing positive social change.* In Psalm 8: 32-35 wisdom speaks further to the faithful who attend with interest to instruction and are blessed by keeping to the proper pathway. There is a warning not to disregard the lessons learned.

Those who listen and are watchful daily at the open door of wisdom will find life and favor from the Lord and will enjoy a missional reality. This is the day for friendship, fellowship, partnership and commitment to constructive social change for the needy of a designated community. This is your opportunity to volunteer for work in a local mission field. This is where you share in God's work and receive His blessing. A simple pledge written many years ago by a previous generation provides guidelines for a quality-of-life bridge to fruitful service. Memorize it and repeat it often.

I solemnly promise to dedicate my life
To the service of God
And to my country.

I will honor my parents, my teachers,
My leaders and my elders,
And those in authority.

I will be clean and honest
In all my thoughts, my words and my deeds.

I will strive, in everything I do,
To work together with my fellowmen
Of every creed and race
For the greater happiness of all,
And the honor and glory of my country.

—Written by Marjorie Padmore and used as an Independence Pledge
for Trinidad & Tobago.

Jesus said, "*Except you are converted and become as a little child, you will not enter the kingdom*" (Matthew 18:3). It would be great if adults could view life and death in a matter-of-fact way as a child does. To be spiritual about life and death one should remember that Scripture instructs that one should weep when a child is born (anticipating life's troubles) and rejoice at death, (the ultimate healing and final victory opens the door to eternal life). Why are these concepts so foreign in our culture?

Mother was getting old and my sister in California kept saying to her family, "I want to move back to Tennessee before mother dies. Some years passed, my sister's children were born, and they received the same message that Nana Green was getting old and was going to die, so they better hurry and move back to Tennessee. Finally, the day came when they all moved back and came to visit mother.

Living alone with no small children around, mother's apartment was filled with nicks n' knacks setting around. When the two young boys began to mess with mother's "stuff," she cautioned them not to break anything. Then one said, *"Oh, it's alright, you're going to die anyway!"* As the family recovered, another boy found mother's pantry. It was a large closet filled with shelves of canned goods that mother kept stocked in case she could not go to the store. The great-grandson asked, *"Nana Green, when you die, can I have your store*?" Children look to the future and give little thought to death. Perhaps faith-based groups should learn from the children and be prepared for life, living, and the afterlife. *"Precious in the sight of the Lord is the death of His saints!"* (Psalms 116:15)

Since death is a part of life and sacred scripture is clear that all must die and face judgment, faith-based groups must realize that salvation is for the whole world. (Hebrews 9:27-28 EDNT) This simply means that the message of grace must get outside the walls of the sanctuary and reach the whole community. This is required to prepare the human race to face life, death and judgment in a right relationship with God. It is not possible to tear down all the houses of worship, but the stained-glass barrier that keeps believers "inside" the building and prevents the use of their "outside voice" must be overcome. This will not happen until believers face their own mortality and become conscious that time is short. They will "go" when they realize that the lost will not "come" to the sanctuary to hear the good news, but the witness must be taken "in living color" to where they are. This should be done at the earliest point in time at the furthest distance from a place of worship. Once individuals are truly converted, they can break the mental barrier and realize the doors to the stained- glass sanctuary are open for the edification of all believers.

Since the Incarnation and the Upper Room experience taught valuable lessons to believers, it is clear that individuals should not be required to cross cultural and linguistic barriers to hear the good news of saving grace in their native language. However, the character and social fabric of each culture and society constructs walls that limit personal expressions of faith. A wall restrains entry and exit of a defined area. Walls which hinder the proper advancement of all who seek life improvement should be removed. Anything that hinders those seeking safety, security or salvation should be taken down.

Since the days of Job, God is no longer in the wall making business. The hedge about Job was taken down, and Satan tried Job sorely, but righteous Job was triumphant in the end. Even evil strategy cannot keep a good man down.

Faith-based walls are man-made barriers that hinder passage in or out of a system of faith. Such a barricade may be based on culture, tradition, or fabricated ideas and values. Normally, ideology walls are permanent structures and belief systems that bar access or expression. Mentally, the adherents are in a prison of previous patterns and have limited access to additional data that would advance their personal faith. Open and free access to faith-based information should be the objective of spiritual leaders. Tragically, sectarian positions remain artificial man-made barriers to a devout and ethical lifestyle for many. We must remove the walls and partitions which separate the people who sincerely desire to worship God.

Among fellow workers it is time for full commitment to a lifestyle that honors God and becomes an example to others.   After a few committed believers did great work for the community of Thessalonica in a few weeks, Paul then journeyed to the next opportunity. Perhaps Paul was aware that "*opportunity equals obligation*." Later he wrote a letter to those who received social and spiritual benefit from the "Together/Strong team" who worked with God on their behalf. Basically, he said "*God was working, and we were together.*"

> *8.Now he who did the planting and the one doing the watering are part of the same process: and every man will receive a reward according to his work. 9.* **For God is working and the laborers are together:** *you are God's farm; you are God's field to be worked and God's building to be constructed. 10. According to the favor of God given to me, as a wise master builder,* **I have laid a foundation, and another will build on it. But let every worker take heed how he builds on the foundation. 11. There is no other foundation for the building but the one on Messiah.** (I Corinthians 3:8-11 EDNT)

> *1.* **As we work together with God, we appeal to you not to accept the grace of God and let it go to waste.** *2. (God said, I have heard your prayers at a convenient time, and in the day of salvation I have brought you relief in a difficult situation:* **observe, now is the time for coming together; now is the day of deliverance**.) (2 Corinthians 6:1-2 EDNT)

Essentially, a missional lifestyle coalesces around a personalized commitment to work with God and a dedicated group on the behalf of others. Such dedication provides a spiritual shift, a sociological direction, and a distinct agenda for sharing benevolence and dignity with the needy. The missional mindset is placed in the context of viewing the Cross through the Empty Tomb, seeing community needs as a vehicle of communication divine love and grace. The committed group becomes a force to work together with God in a designated community. **You have been chosen by God, to be part of the Together/ Strong NETWORK to work with others and intensify positive social change.**

> ...I have chosen you and appointed you to go out and bring in fruit, and that your fruit should remain and that you should obtain answers to your prayers to make them fruitful. 17. These things I command you, so that you may love one another. (John 15:16-17 EDNT)

What is the missional mindset? What does a missionary know and how do they feel about the people to whom God sends them to do both humanitarian service and moral guidance? They know beyond a doubt they have been called to serve outside their comfort zone. They understand they must leave behind some family and friends and travel into an unfamiliar place. They are aware of different languages, cultures, traditions and even strange faith-based systems they will encounter. They will face hardship and loneliness. Such souls know they must live a life worthy of financial and prayerful support from an extended constituency. They know they have limited resources and that through deputation they must raise and replace funds that are spent, or they cannot continue their work. This provides a totally different perspective on money matters. A family involved in missions cultivates a positive mindset that God is in charge of their lives and ministry. Missionaries must teach their children to live on a limited budget and that every dollar and each cent saved enhances their chance of blooming where God has planted them to reach others with love and grace.

> **Sidebar:** after traveling to Ecuador when the five missionaries were killed, many lessons were learned that time and space would not permit sharing here. The point relative to this chapter is my letter with a sister of Nate Saint, who returned to Ecuador to serve the same Indians who killed her brother. She was asked, "How can you work as a Missionary with those who killed your brother? Her answer to my question was an admonishment not to use a capital "M" for missionary. She clearly shared …*all believers are "missionaries", and the word should never be capitalized.* Her dedication and guidance altered my education, teaching and in my philosophy of missions and ministry through education in over 100 countries. Even after 65 years there remains hesitation about capitalizing words such as, pastor, minister, deacon, elder, etc. because …*all believers are to function as "missionaries."*

How does a missional lifestyle fit with positive social change? When one is asked to accept an assignment to improve a needy community where they live, work or worship; it is best that they adopt the thinking, behaviors, and practices of a missionary in order to fully comprehend the nature of what they are being asked to do. Committed missionaries are willing to go outside their comfort zone and encounter difficulties not of their own making. They see beneficial change as not only humanitarian community service, but also a service to some who are following the wrong path in life because of bad influence, a deficient family, faith-based worship and/or community environment. A missionary sees every soul as a prospect for love and grace. They are aware *that the children already belong to God and are under His watch care 24/7/365. Children are a gift from God, and they need assistance and opportunity equals obligation.*

Your task as part of the Together/Strong TEAM is to construct a **Quality-of-Life Bridge as a Silver Lining for life's cloudy days.**

Quality of Life Bridge

ALPHA — CARE FOR THE CHILDREN

OMEGA — CARE FOR THE ELDERLY

BRIDGE OVER TROUBLED WATER

ADULTS

Quality is determined by attitudes and actions

Ultimately quality increases the quantity of life

Activities to ensure that daily life has value

Living a useful life produces true happiness

Intervention to adjust areas of discontent

Total life assessment to assure positive living

Yielding gracefully to ageing and the future

Opportunity to grow and develop personally

Faithfulness in all personal and social relationships

Learning and sharing with others

Increasing the worth of friends

Future healthy and comfortable state

Evaluates and encourage a sense of well-being

Builds passageways to a better outlook on life

Renewing personal and social commitments

Improved intentionality of personal action

Developing problem-solving and social skills

Growing older with dignity and self-respect

Enjoying the stages of life without regret

— From Ramjattan, Subesh. (2018)
Ageing has a Silver Lining. ISBN 979-1-935434-65-8.
A capstone of his work with the disadvantaged.

Life After Birth

In a mother's womb were two babies. ***One asked the other:***

"Do you believe in life after delivery?" **The other replied,** *"Why, of course. There has to be something after delivery. Maybe we are here to prepare ourselves for what we will be later."*

"Nonsense" **said the first**. *"There is no life after delivery. What kind of life would that be?"*

The second said, *"I don't know, but there will be more light than here. Maybe we will walk with our legs and eat from our mouths. Maybe we will have other senses that we can't understand now."*

The first replied, *"That is absurd. Walking is impossible. And eating with our mouths? Ridiculous! The umbilical cord supplies nutrition and everything we need. But the umbilical cord is so short. Life after delivery is to be logically excluded."*

The second insisted, *"Well I think there is something and maybe it's different than it is here. Maybe we won't need this physical cord anymore."*

The first replied, *"Nonsense. And more over if there is life, then why has no one ever come back from there? Delivery is the end of life, and in the after-delivery there is nothing but darkness and silence and oblivion. It takes us nowhere."*

"Well, I don't know," said **the second**, *"but certainly we will meet Mother and she will take care of us."*

The first replied *"Mother? You actually believe in Mother? That's laughable. If Mother exists, then where is She now?"*

The second said, "She is all around us. We are surrounded by her. We are of Her. It is in Her that we live. Without Her this world would not and could not exist."

Said the first: *"Well I don't see Her, so it is only logical that She doesn't exist."*

To which the second replied, "Sometimes, when you're in silence and you focus and you really listen, you can perceive Her presence, and you can hear Her loving voice, calling down from above."

—Attributed to Hungarian writer
Útmutató a Léleknek

About the Author

Hollis L. Green, ThD, PhD, DLitt, is a Clergy-Educator with public relations and business credentials and doctorates in theology, education, and philosophy. A Distinguished Professor of Education and Social Change at the graduate level for over four decades, Dr. Green is a Diplomate in the Oxford Society of Scholars, and author of 50+ books. He served six years as a member of the U.S. Senate Business Advisory Board and maintained certified membership in several public relations societies (RPRC, PRSA, and IPRC). He served pastorates in five states, a Military Chaplain during the Vietnam era, a denominational official for 18 years, and traveled and lectured in over 100 countries.

Dr. Green was the founder (1974) A.I.D. Ltd., Associated Institutional Developers, Ltd. (an international Public Relations and Corporate Consultant Company). He was Vice-President (1974-1979) Luther Rice Seminary (www.lru.edu); the founding President (1981) and Chancellor (1991-2008) of Oxford Graduate School, and Chancellor Emeritus [www.ogs.edu]. As part of a global outreach, Dr. Green founded (2002) OASIS University in Trinidad, West Indies [www.oasisgradedu.org] where he continues to serve as a Professor of Education and Social Change and Chancellor.

In 2004, he assisted in establishing Greenleaf Educational Foundation in Colorado to advance higher education.

In addition to other endeavors, Dr. Green launched Global Educational Advance, Inc. and GEA Press (2007) [www.gea-books.com] to advance higher education and positive social change through publishing, curriculum advance, library/learning resources, improved instruction, and global book distribution. His books and assisting authors in publishing are a logical outgrowth of a sixty-year service through education. He serves Global as Corporate Chair and Co-publisher with his sons, Barton and Brian. Dr. Green continues to speak, teach, write books and work with authors in publishing quality creative work.

Afterword

Guidance for Sociological Change

Constructive social change requires both right thinking and right doing. The structure of social change provides workable ways to observe a community, social scientific means of gathering data, and practical ways of opening the hearts and minds and permitting small changes to flow. Then when small changes are accepted making them a permanent part of the cultural milieu.

In social theory one learns that individuals change more rapidly than groups, institutions and societies. An affirmative attitude is needed to make a difference, but legislation or outside imposed adjustments or alterations will not be readily accepted. The reasons and rationale must come from community residents to be within the *bounds of acceptance.* Individuals are the persons who can change; consequently, change advocates must listen to the personal expression of long- term residents.

Leadership is the ability to influence others to follow one voluntarily toward stated goals, but this must not be pushed: individuals must *voluntarily* follow. It is gentle guidance that influence change and changed individuals are able to prompt group change. Then, small groups with an altered mindset may encourage change in the community of which they are apart. Eventually, society would feel the force of gradual constructive change.

When it is gradual change over time, change will be accepted and even embraced. Most prefer instant change, but social change is sequential and incremental over time. Perseverance and open-mindedness are required to maintain the flow of change and solidify the final integration of modifications into the culture and lifestyle of the people.

> **Sidebar:** Segregation began before the USA was a Nation. In the decade of 1860, the States fought a Civil War and Lincoln signed the Emancipation Proclamation to free slaves. On March 30, 1870 the Fifteenth Amendment was ratified: *"The rights of citizens of the United States to vote shall not be denied or abridged by the United States or any State on account of race, color, or previous condition of Servitude."* The following day, May 31, 1870, President Ulysses S. Grant signed the first Enforcement Act that substantially secured the voting rights of freedmen. One year later, President Grant signed the Second Enforcement Act (1871) to protect black suffrage and targeted the activities of violent groups that resisted the progress. About five years later, President Grant signed the Civil Rights Act of 1875. This ground-breaking act prohibited segregation in various modes of public accommodations and transportation and discrimination in jury selection.

President Grant's role in securing the political equality of all Citizens regardless of color is unequaled in US history. Even after the popular will overwhelmingly turned against the Grant's efforts to protect the political and civil rights of former slaves. Grant refused to abandon his commitment to the freedom for which he had fought. After he left office, the South was allowed to enter a new era of disfranchisement. During this period, President Grant's efforts to protect the freedmen during Reconstruction were widely ridiculed and declared to be misguided. Such criticism has weakened in the face of history.

About 100 years later in the decade of 1960, during assignations and civil disturbance, President Johnson signed more Civil Rights Legislation. With patience and tolerance, perhaps in the decade of 2060, the USA will develop a color-blind society and begin to function as a melting pot rather than a stew pot.

This is hopeful anticipation based on the social theory timetable, but it should be remembered that discrimination and slavery did not begin with the Colonies or the Confederacy. It began in the evil minds and greedy souls of people around the world who chose to look down on someone because they perceived them-selves to be superior. Slavery was not a sociological project; it was aggressive trade and personal greed to take advantage of a situation for the benefit of a few and the detriment of generations. This discrimination built legal walls and social fences and created false barriers to human social progress in housing, education, the labor market and the professions. Some remnants of discrimination remain which create roadblocks to social progress based on culture, race, language and worship.

Some members of the minority have personally risen above the fray and been assisted over the wall and through the maze to a better life, but most individuals with minority status have been hindered in their personal and social progress. Some of the roadblocks have been in conservative politics, within religious community, among community leaders, and sometimes within the minority itself. Some have said that weekly worship is the most segregated time of the week. Perhaps this is true, but is it enforced or by choice and culture? When social integration works in education, housing, and the workplace, why is weekly worship still segregated? It is by choice based on cultural heritage.

> **Sidebar:** One of my doctoral students (Robert L. Allen, 1987) at Oxford Graduate School did a study to see whether the progress of social integration would hinder the survival of Black Churches. When three indices were compared: Social Integration Index, Black Church Participation Index, and Black Heritage Index, the level of social integration made no difference in participation. Only the Black Heritage Index made a significant difference. The higher the Black Heritage index the more apt one was to participate in ethnic-based worship. It was not segregation; it was cultural heritage which drew them to the worship and to the music that fit their culture. So, it is possible for a minority group to be integrated socially, economically, and educationally and still maintain an ethnic-based worship. After all most of the local churches and all the denominations have a cultural control indicator. This is not a justification for worship segregation, or accepting divisions in faith-based groups; it the statement of a sociological fact. And perhaps an explanation of how it has happened. In fact, it is the minorities that continue this separation as part of their cultural expression of heritage. The same dynamics cause some to attend a synagogue, a mosque, or a Baptist or Methodist service. This will change over time, but it will change on its own, not by external forces or even gentle persuasion. Perchance the Pandemic of 2020 and the political upheaval will open the door for movement toward change: good and bad.

As the essential elements of personal faith, not the sectarian dogma, are integrated into the social fabric of a community, there will be a gradual change. Only a drastic change of the heart, a spiritual renewal of the soul, could speed up the process. Heritage and tradition are big components of social resistance to change.

Heritage becomes a legacy passed on by tradition to the next generation. At times it may be perpetuated by inheritance factors when family elders have traditionally been associated with a particular institution or ethnic based worship experience, the young may feel obligated or privileged to follow the same path. Most want to hold on to the memories and the subconscious imprinting of the past. The more this difficulty is understood, the better society will be in accepting the gradual social change that is predictable.

A cultural framework for establishing sectarian positions has been the norm in most places of worship. Faith-based groups developed congregations out of historical and cultural roots. It appears that cultural foundations can identify most, if not all denominational groups. These cultural and regional origins have colored various interpretations of sacred writings and transformed others to meet their personal beliefs. Over time these various interpretations and teachings were given brand names and promoted as the correct and proper way to worship and find peace, happiness, and a positive afterlife. Most religious groups and divisions can be traced to cultural roots or national origins.

There is no question about the three monotheistic faiths: Judaism, Christianity and Islam. The Eastern religions are also culturally based. Within each of these Faith structures there are differences based on leaders and culture. The divisions of Christianity are obviously influenced by aspects of culture and regional heritage.

Most are culturally branded by name. The Roman Catholic identity is obvious. The Church of England, the Greek and Russian Orthodox Churches have obvious national influence. Methodist and Episcopal groups have English beginnings, Presbyterians have Scottish roots, Lutherans have foundations in Germany, Baptists have European beginnings, and the list goes on. At one time in America, there was even a Swedish Baptist Church. That particular group changed its identity when it ran out of Swedes. Religious groups have created places of worship clustered around sectarian constructs with brand names that have identified and advanced a particular view as an accurate interpretation of sacred writings. This generated isolated, sectarian groups with a sense of exclusivity.

When the young are taught these traditions, it is difficult to make meaningful change or produce a spirit of cooperation among the various perspectives. Facts are viewed through cultural glasses and the interpretations differ from group to group. Consequently, universal truth became the exclusive domain of a faith-based authority and shared only with a limited or carefully chosen constituency. Various teachings and different doctrine were culturally interpreted but firmly and authoritatively proclaimed as the true and proper expression of the inspired scriptural writings. In spite of this complexity, some have found and do worship God in their cultural clothes and traditions.

While Judaism, the Roman Catholics, members of Islam and the Protestant community accentuated various differences as a badge of honor, each group behaves as if they have found the "Holy Grail" and have exclusive access to the "secrets" of faith and practice. This facilitates exclusive attitudes and encourages division within families and communities. It also hinders broad constructive social change.

Judaism has small internal differences, but the Jewish community maintains a unified identity. When individuals are identified as being Jewish, one immediately has an idea of their basic values. Judaism has a sense of community and commitment to the individual and family. The public understands much of the essential elements of Jewish worship and family values. Although some differences exist among Roman Catholics, they manage to present a unified voice to the average citizen. Other faith-based groups, such as Islam, Mormons and Jehovah's Witnesses manage to overcome differences and present a common identity. This is not true of most protestant communions.

This greatly complicates the integration of moral principles into society. *"Can two walk together except they agree?"* Some basic moral principles and religious experiences would enhance the acceptance among minorities and greatly advance caring for one's neighbor and loving one another in true acts of human kindness. Yet, many human beings are normally prejudiced.

A three-day countercultural festival at Woodstock (1969) occurred when religiosity was important in the lives of seventy (70) percent of citizens of the United States. While faith-based leaders and a silent majority were preparing for their children to return to public education, one Reporter described Woodstock as *"an open, classless society of music, sex, drugs, love and peace."*

Woodstock challenged the conservative views of the majority. However, fifty (50) years later the Gallup group reported a survey of the major ways **public norms and circumstances joined with the Woodstock mindset to influence drastic social change.** The Vietnam War, civil strife, movements for gender and racial equality, the explosive advance of technology, multiple TV's, cell phones, personal computers with access to the Internet and social media have accelerated change in family life, the workplace, governmental operations, and personal space.

Unintended consequences of these influences in social change have compounded complex attitudes and created an unexpected acceptance of controversial changes. Woodstock was not the direct cause for changes in the social norms, but it was a wake-up call for parents and the moral majority to which they turned a deaf ear. This obvious failure was compounded by the consequences of changes in the social and political environment over the next five decades. These changes have been far-reaching and seem to be irreversible.

In addition to decline in the view *"that religion was very important"* from 70% to 52 % in 2019 among Americans, the willingness to legalize certain drugs has increased from 31% to 66% in the past two decades. Racial tolerance and interracial marriage acceptance increased to nearly 90%. Gay Rights are supported by 71% of Americans on the basis of Civil Rights and equal justice. Civil Rights Laws and affirmative action made a small difference for some in the level of overt discrimination and injustice, but not in the core attitude of a majority. There are still those in the majority that either accept the whole and reject the part or accept the part and reject the whole. Whether gender, racial or lifestyle, what is needed is an affirmative attitude toward all whose attitude and behavior differs from the majority.

The articulation of an assenting approach to responsible change, lawful behavior, and the attitude of a good neighbor should come from a positive predisposition to behave with personal moral responsibly. It would be useful for social change if people were tolerant of others. However, tolerance is not complete acceptance

Abortion has increased in the first trimester and a majority continue to support legalized abortion based on the mother's health and the viability of the fetus based on birth defects and/or a failure to normally develop for sustainability after birth. In addition, the case for women's reproductive rights and the growing population of the world have caused a marked change in family size. Yet, many homeless children are on the streets without safety, shelter or sustenance with no assurance of a "home" or adequate parenting. This does not bode well for the next cycle of community leaders.

Political attitudes have changed to a willingness to vote for government leadership regardless of gender 94% or race 96%. Also, the glass ceiling has been shattered for politics, higher education, religion and business. Almost three-fourths no longer oppose premarital sex. What will be the consequence for marriage, family life and the offspring of such unions?

An aggressive immorality seems to be growing with almost no resistance. It appears the global society has turned backward on itself and deteriorated into the social and human debauchery of the Greco-Roman pagan state and is moving toward a repeat of the historic darkness that followed Roman paganism. This system deified leaders, warriors, actors and musicians, and neglected family, human rights, community values, and a sense of personal faith until the whole Empire deteriorated into progressive immorality and self-indulgence.

God wants His Creation back and
all humans filled with faith and love
for their fellowman.

Jesus wants His brand identity back
and prayer restored in His follower's lives.
He desires His rightful place as
Head of the Houses of Worship.

The Spirit is grieved by the lifestyle of
believers as He continues working
to convict the world of sin,
righteousness and judgment.
A Creator God does not dwell in
man-made buildings, but
in the living souls of His disciples.

Appendix A

The Abrupt End of Acts

Why the abrupt end of the Acts of the Apostles? The Acts of the Holy Spirit through the early messengers of Jesus does not have a close; it is assumed that all believers and each local congregation are to continue writing the history of God working through individuals enabled by the Spirit. The big question is: what has God done in your life or place of worship lately worthy of recording in such a book? Below are possible explanations for this abrupt ending:

1. Luke intended to write a sequel. Luke deliberately wrote books and may have planned to do another volume of pristine church history.

2. The Holy Spirit desired that each person in each generation should keep written journals or a record of God's dealing with them, their family, friends and congregation. If this were done, their journal would read similar to a chapter in the Acts. Would it not be wonderful if each believer had a record of God's intervention in their personal lives, answered prayers, spiritual enablement for special tasks, and the general working of the Holy Spirit in their local assembly? During times of trouble or despair, the reading of such a record would be a source of spiritual encouragement. Memories are often short and fading, a written record would be an authentic record of spiritual blessings.

3. There was actually another chapter to Luke's account, but it was lost or left out of the canon of scripture for some reason. Any serious student of Biblical languages:

(Hebrew and Greek) can easily see that different manuscripts, translations, and versions of sacred writings have differences that could be attributed to human error or intentional omission. Just as individuals today twist and misinterpret scripture to justify their personal beliefs, it could be that some additions and omissions from scripture were intentional.

4. A view in certain quarters of England is the idea that the Anglo-Saxon peoples are the lost ten tribes of Israel who were carried into captivity by Assyria in 722 B.C., and never heard of since. There is a historical record of a long-lost chapter (29) of the Acts of the Apostles, containing the account of Paul's journey to Spain and Britain. Naturally, the authenticity of the document is in question. The text made its first appearance in London in 1871. According to the editor, it was translated in the late 18th century by the French naturalist Sonnini de Manoncourt from a Greek manuscript discovered in the archives at Constantinople and presented to him by the Sultan Abdoul Achmet. It was discovered in an English translation of Sonnini's Voyage en Grèce et en Turquie in the library of Sir John Newport, MP (1756-1843) after Newport's death. However, no evidence of such a manuscript has been found, and from internal evidence, cultural anthropology considers it most likely to be a hoax, and is classified among the writings of disputed authenticity of which some were included in the Vulgate and Septuagint, but not in the Hebrew or Protestant canon. However, it is an example of what could have happened following the abrupt close of Acts Chapter 28. It is presented here simply as an illustration not as an authentic or authorized part of Acts.

A Possible Lost Chapter of Acts (29). *29:1-26*

1. And Paul, full of the blessings of Christ, and abounding in the spirit, departed out of Rome, determining to go into Spain, for he had a long time proposed to journey there, and was minded also to go from thence to Britain. 2. For he had heard in Phoenicia that certain of the children of Israel, about the time of the Assyrian captivity, had escaped by sea to "the Isles afar off" as spoken by the Prophet, and called by the Romans, Britain. 3. And the Lord commanded the gospel to be preached far hence to the Gentiles, and to the lost sheep of the House of Israel. 4. And no man hindered Paul; for he testified boldly of Jesus before the tribunes and among the people; and he took with him certain of the brethren which abode with him at Rome, and they took shipping at Ostrium and having the winds fair, were brought safely into a haven of Spain. 5. And much people were gathered together from the towns and villages, a the hill country; for they had heard of the conversion to the Apostle, and the many miracles which he had wrought. 6. And Paul preached mightily in Spain, and great multitudes believed and were converted, for they perceived he was an apostle sent from God. 7. And they departed out of Spain, and Paul and his company finding a ship in Armorica sailing unto Britain, they were therein, and passing along the south Coast, they reached a port called Raphinus. 8. Now when it was voiced abroad that the Apostle had landed on their coast, great multitudes of the inhabitants met him, and they treated Paul courteously and he entered in at the east gate of their city, and lodged in the house of an Hebrew and one of his own nation. 9. And on the morrow he came and stood upon Mount Lud and the people thronged at the gate, and assembled in the Broadway, and he preached Christ unto them, and they believed the Word and the testimony of Jesus. 10. And at even the Holy Ghost fell upon Paul, and he prophesied, saying, Behold, in the last days the

God of Peace shall dwell in the cities, and the inhabitants thereof shall be numbered: and in the seventh numbering of the people, their eyes shall be opened, and the glory of their inheritance shine forth before them. The nations shall come up to worship on the mount that testified of the patience and long suffering of a servant of the Lord. 11. And in the latter days new tidings of the Gospel shall issue forth out of Jerusalem, and the hearts of the people shall rejoice, and behold, fountains shall be opened, and there shall be no more plague. 12. In those days there shall be wars and rumors of war; and a king shall rise up, and his sword, shall be for the healing of the nations, and his peacemaking shall abide, and the glory of his kingdom a wonder among princes. 13. And it came to pass that certain of the Druids came unto Paul privately, and showed by their rites and ceremonies they were descended from the Jews which escaped from bondage in the land of Egypt, and the apostle believed these things, and he gave them the kiss of friendship. And Paul abode in his lodgings three months confirming in the faith and preaching Christ continually. 15. And after these things Paul and his brethren departed from Raphinus, and sailed unto Atium in Gaul. 16. And Paul preached in the Roman garrison and among the people, exhorting all men to repent and confess their sins. 17. And there came to him certain of the Belgae to enquire of him of the new doctrine, and of the man Jesus; And Paul opened his heart unto them and told them all things that had befallen him, howbeit, that Christ Jesus came into the world to save sinners; and they departed pondering among themselves upon the things which they had eard.18. And after much preaching and toil, Paul and his fellow laborers passed into Helvetia, and came to Mount Pontius Pilate, where he who condemned the Lord Jesus dashed himself down headlong, and so miserably perished. 19. Immediately a torrent gushed out of the mountain and washed his body, broken in pieces, into a lake. 20. And Paul stretched forth his hands upon the water, and prayed unto the Lord, saying O Lord God, give a sign unto all nations that here Pontius Pilate which condemned your only begotten son, plunged down headlong into the pit. 21. And while Paul was yet speaking, behold, there came a great earthquake, and the face of the waters was changed, and the form of the lake like unto the Son of Man hanging in an agony upon the Cross. 22. And a voice came out of heaven saying, Even Pilate hath escaped the wrath to come for he washed his hands before the multitude at the blood-shedding of the Lord Jesus. 23. When, therefore, Paul and those that were with him saw the earthquake, and heard the voice of the angel, they glorified God, they were mightily strengthened in the spirit. 24. And they journeyed and came to Mount Julius where stood two pillars, one on the right hand and one on the left hand, erected by Caesar Augustus. 25. And Paul, filled with the Holy Ghost, stood up between the two pillars, saying, Men and brethren these stones which ye see this day shall testify of my journey hence, and verily I say, they shall remain until the outpouring of the spirit upon all nations, neither shall the way be hindered throughout all generations. 26. And they went forth and came unto Illtricum, intending to go by Macedonia into Asia, and grace was found in all the assemblies, and they prospered and had peace. Amen!

Note: The big question is not the authenticity of this document (Acts 29), but what has God done in your life or place of worship lately worthy of a preserved record to authenticate spiritual leadership and activity in obedience to the Challenge of Jesus in Matthew 28:16-20?

Appendix B

Operational Definitions

Communications – the passing of information from one person to another regardless of the means. It involves sharing with another in active participation, a kind of give and take exchange. To communicate there must be a sender and a receiver using common encoding and decoding. Plus they have to overcome the static of the environment.

Community – is a gathering of individuals sharing common rights and privileges or interests and living under the same laws and regulations. It suggests mutual association on equal and friendly terms. The word suggests familiarity.

Contextual Analysis – separating a whole into parts to find their nature, proportion, function, and relationship in order to weave together a new integrated whole.

Constructive Change – positive movement in the direction of modification and adjustments to make the general atmosphere and reality better for all.

Culture – the ancestral background, beliefs, family values, practices, social order and collective achievements as a social group.

Faith-based – belief system and commitment to honor and worship a Higher Power based on specific sacred or historical writings.

Ideology and Change – a formation in the affective domain where ideas and values of an individual or class are derived exclusively through feelings. One's theology and philosophy create their ideology based on ideas and values. These values and ideas that are used to produce change.

Identity – an understanding of personal roles based on philosophy, theology, tradition and culture.

Integration – to make whole or new by adding or bringing together parts. The study of theology and/or philosophy creates one's value system and ideology. At the level of ideology and values, different individuals and divergent groups find common ground to effect social change in society.

Interpretation – a constructive effort to explain meaning or express a personal conception, version, or rendition of someone or something.

Multicultural Society – a heterogeneous mixture of ethnicity and social order that exists in many parts or forms and holds that reality is composed of a multiplicity of principles based on ancestral background and traditional behavior and values

Orthopraxis – trusting the best practices and methodological operation of sociology.

Philosophy – a study of the processes governing thought and conduct including aesthetics, ethics, logic, metaphysics, morals, character and behavior.

Philosophical theory – that reality is made up of many kinds of being or substance

Pluralistic – existence of different groups within society: cultural, ethnic, language, religious, or political differences.

Sociological – the structure, function and development of human society.

Sociology policy or theory – that minority groups within a society should maintain cultural difference, but share overall political and economic power

Social Change – human interactions and relationships that transform cultural and social groups over time

Social Problem – an obvious area of concern by individuals or groups that has an antecedent cause and present negative consequence for the environment and human habitation.

Theology – a study of the relationship between God and humanity as to matters of religious dogma. Basically what "others" believe and say about sacred writings.

Appendix C

Other Books by the Author

To understand the problems of faith-based entities and advance delivery systems for graduate education, extensive research was done during the past two decades. Meanwhile, his schedule was filled with academic administration, teaching, research and writing, but colleagues and friends have encouraged sequels to his best-known works. In the post-retirement years, Dr. Green followed that prompt and produced twenty (20+) books plus ten Children's Novellas.

- ► *Why Churches Die.* (2007) ISBN 978-1-9796019-03 A fresh assessment of congregational vitality to determine thirty-five reasons why faith-based congregations were losing their pristine power of outreach.

- ► *Interpreting an Author's Words.* (2008) ISBN 978-0980-164-74—Define both formal and informal study and writing skills by understanding how to clearly interpret the spoken and written words of others.

- ► *Titanic Lesson.* (2008) ISBN 978-0-9796019-6-5 An answer to the question: "Do historic realities predict problems for a growing faith-based group?

- ► *Sympathetic Leadership Cybernetics.* (2010) ISBN 978-1-9354345-28 – This work attempts to clarify management and leadership in the context of organizational and institutional functionality and charts a course for organizations to serve the needs of people through shepherd management and servant leadership.

- ► *Why Christianity Fails in America.* (2010) ISBN 978-0-9796019-10 -- A call for an internal redirection of the heart and soul to make the pristine faith viable in the Twenty-first century.

▶ ***How to Build a Better Spouse Trap.*** (2010) ISBN 978-1—9354344-50 – A major failure of faith-based groups is they have made little difference in the lives of individuals and their function in the family. How to choose a mate, learn from our mistakes, stay married, and teach others to break the cycle of dysfunctional relationships. The family unit is a microcosm of faith-based behavior.

▶ ***Discipleship.*** (2010) ISBN 978-0-9796019-5-8 A revived edition to better explain the process of a believer's lifestyle from conversion (change direction), to discipleship (learning), to apostle (mature enough to be trusted with the message of grace.)

▶ ***SO TALES.*** (2011) ISBN 978-1-9354345-80 -- Preserving 240 true stories from the past for the benefit of family and friends.

▶ ***Designing Valid Research.*** (2011) ISBN 978-1-9354345-73 – A guide to designing a research proposal and developing a social scientific dissertation.

▶ ***Titanic Lessons.*** (2012) ISBN 978-0-9796019-6-5 – An effort to demonstrate that bigger is not necessarily better and that all building of machines, organizations, and institutions must use material that meets the precise requirements of the task. This must be applied to people, process, and functionality of the human element and the mechanics must match the environment.

▶ ***Why Wait Till Sunday?*** (2012) ISBN 978-1-935434-27-6- A renewal plan for older congregations who depended on programs coming down from sectarian authority rather than locally generated ideas and involvement in seven (7) aspects of renewal.

- ▶ *Fighting the Amalekites.* (2013)
  ISBN 978-1-935434-30-6 – The unhealthy addictions, unproductive habits, an uncontrolled tongue are all little "Amalekites"; unless these are destroyed they will become the destroyer. These join the Amalekites that ambush and take advantage of spiritual weaknesses.

- ▶ *Remedial and Surrogate Parenting* (2013) 2nd Ed.
  ISBN 978-1-9354344-81--*A Resource for Parents, Teachers, and Childcare Services.* Children are a gift of God and a legacy of faith-based families; therefore, parenting skills are essential This work is guidance for remedial human development (0-20).

- ▶ *Transformational Leadership in Education.* (2013) 2nd Ed. ISBN 978-1-9354342-38-- A strengths-based approach to education for administrators, teachers, and guidance counselors.

- ▶ *Tear Down These Walls.* (2013)
  ISBN 978-1-9354341-84 -- A priority agenda must be to make people moral citizens of the world before they can become mystical citizens of heaven. Where organized groups choose not to function, personal action could make a difference and break down some of the barriers that divide the faith-based community and strengthen the "One Lord-One Faith–One Baptism" message.

- ▶ *The EVERGREEN Devotional New Testament – C.A.F.E. Edition.* (2015, 2018)
  ISBN 978-1-9354342-69 – EDNT is a 42-year project to translate common NT Greek and determine the meaning "then" and how words can best be expressed "now" and remain true to the original intent expressed in a common devotional language.

- ▶ *Recycled Words n' Stuff.* (2016)
  ISBN 978-1-9354348-63 – A collection of short narratives and essays of general interest.

- ***The Children's Bread** – Unlocking whole life stewardship* (2018) ISBN 978-1-935434-90-0– *Appreciating faith-based economics and personal wealth to unlock a missional lifestyle and founding for humanitarian and faith-based entities.*

- ***Kingdom Growth Through Missional Behavior*** (2019)—*adopting the thinking, behaviors, and practices of a missionary in order to globalize the message of grace.* ISBN 978-1-935434-91-7

- ***God Has Confidence in You*** (2019) ISBN 98-1-950839-04-9. No test has come your way but such as is common to man: God is faithful, who will not permit you to be tested beyond your endurance; but will with each test also show you a way forward, so that you may be victorious.

- ***Power of Forgiveness and Reconciliation*** (2020) – *Forgiveness is the sunrise of reconciliation.* ISBN 978-1-950839-06-3

- ***Beyond Pulpit, Classroom and Lecture Hall*** (2020) *Unlocking Exposition, Instruction and Research Reporting in Subject Matter Sharing.* ISBN 978-1-950839-03-2

- ***Navigating Multiculturalism*** (2021) *Guidance for Sociological Change ISBN 978-1-950839-10-0*

Plus these children's books, in keeping with the Dons of Oxford University:

- ***Sleepy Town Lullaby and Story*** - (2008) ISBN 978-0-9796019-4-1

- ***The Scoop about Birthday Soup*** - (2008) ISBN 978-0-97960198-9

- *The Funky Chicken's Wedding;*

- *Cranky Not-so-Hottra'*

- *Cat-Astropic Charlie;*

- *A Tea Party at Nany's House;*
- *The Shimonaka Big Dripper;*
- *The Mouse of the House;*
- *The Boy Who Wanted to Grow a Beard;*
- *The Trouble with Funny Book Cussing;*
- *The Blue Jay and Grandma's Song;*
- *Ditala Killed a Dead Snake*

Books in Process

Research Methods for Problem Solvers and Critical Thinkers. (2021) —Guidance in developing a master's thesis, designing a doctoral research proposal and constructing a defendable dissertation based on social scientific research with an objective of positive social change. ISBN 978-1-935434-92-4

All Believers Are Created Equal. (2021) – *Developing the Path to Moral Excellence.* (Based on 2 Peter Chapter One). – ISBN 978-1-950839-11-7

THE POWER SERIES   *(21 volumes)*

1. **Power of Forgiveness and Reconciliation**
    ISBN 978-1-950839-06-3   [2020]
2. Power of Prayer and Perseverance
3. Power of Lordship and Worship
4. Power of Giving and Receiving
5. Power of Lifestyle and Witness
6. Power of Mission and Going
7. Power of Fellowship and Friends
8. Power of Assimilation and Application
9. Power of Learning and Sharing
10. Power of Planting and Harvest

11. Power of Hunger and Pursuit
12. Power of Longevity and Legacy
13. Power of Enthusiasm and Affirmation
14. Power of Camaraderie and Companions
15. Power of Hearth and Home
16. Power of Confession and Communion
17. Power of Purpose and Timetable
18. Power of Faith and Moral Excellence
19. Power Scarcity and Abundance
20. Power of Connectivity and Friendship
21. Power of Love and Hate

www.gea-books.com
or anywhere good books are sold.

The EVERGREEN Devotional New Testament (EDNT)

Available for this title:

Hardcover ISBN 978-1-935434-28-3

Softcover ISBN 978-1-935434-26-9

eBook ISBN 978-1-935434-74-0

Reference Bibliography

Babbie, Earl. (2001). *The Practice of Social Research* (9th edition) Wadsworth/Thompson Learning.

Bailey, Kenneth D. (2006). *Living Systems Theory and Social Entropy Theory*. Systems Research and Behavioral Science, 22, 291-300.

Balloo, Paratan (2018). *Leadership Theory & Social Change --Formal and Informal Aspects of Leadership in Organizations.* Nashville: GlobalEdAdvancePress.

Berger, R.M., & Patchner, M.A. (1988). *Planning for Research: A Guide for the Helping Professions*. Newbury Park, CA: Sage.

Behrens, L. (1992). *The American Experience: A Sourcebook for Critical Thinking and Writing*. Boston: Allyn and Bacon.

Bloom B. S. (1956).*Taxonomy of Educational Objectives, Handbook I: The Cognitive Domain*. New York: David McKay Co Inc.

Brockett, R. G. & Hiemstra, R. (1991) *Self-Direction in Adult Learning: Perspectives on Theory, Research, and Practice*, London and New York: Routledge.

Bryman, Alan. (2008). *Social Research Methods*. Oxford University Press.

Candy, Philip C. 1991. *Self-Direction for Lifelong Learning*. San Francisco:

Crosby, B.C. (1999). *Leadership for Global Citizenship: Building Transnational Community*. Thousand Oaks, CA: Sage Publications.

Drucker, F. Peter. (1995). *Managing in a Time of Great Change*. New York: Penguin Group.

Glaser, Edward M. (1941). *An Experiment in the Development of Critical Thinking*. Volmnis zu.

Giles, C. (2006). *Transformational Leadership in Challenging Urban Elementary Schools: A role For Parental Involvement?* University of Buffalo, The State University of New York.

Green, Hollis Lynn (2008). *Interpreting An Author's Words*, Nashville: GlobalEdAdvancePress.

Green, Hollis L. (2010) *Sympathetic Leadership Cybernetics*, GlobalEdAdvancePress. Nashville.

Green, Hollis L. (2010) *Why Christianity Fails in America*. GlobalEdAdvancePress. Nashville.

Green, Hollis L. (2011). *Designing Valid Research*. GlobalEdAdvancePress. Nashville

Green, Hollis L. (2013) *Remedial and Surrogate Parenting*. GlobalEdAdvancePress. Nashville.

Green, Hollis L. (2018). *The Evergreen Devotional New Testament* C.A.F.E. Edition, Post-Gutenberg Books. Nashville.

Green, Hollis L. (2018) *The Children's Bread* – Unlocking whole life stewardship: Accessing faith-based economics and personal wealth

Green, Hollis L. & Jackson, Basil. (2019) *Kingdom Growth Through Missional Behavior* — Adopting the thinking, behaviors, and practices of a missionary in order to globalize the message of grace GlobalEdAdvancePress. Nashville.

Green, Hollis L. & Ramjattan, Subesh (2019) *God Has Confidence in You* — No test has come your way, but such as is common to man: God is faithful, who will not permit you to be tested beyond your endurance; but will with each test also show you a way forward, so that you may be victorious. GlobalEdAdvancePress. Nashville.

Green, Hollis L. (2020) *Power of Forgiveness and Reconciliation* — Forgiveness is the Sunrise of Reconciliation. GlobalEdAdvancePress. Nashville.

Green, Hollis L. (2020) *Beyond Pulpit, Classroom and Lecture Hall* — Unlocking Exposition, Instruction and Research Reporting in Subject Matter. GlobalEdAdvancePress. Nashville.

Gutek, Gerald Lee, (1988). *Philosophical and Ideological Perspectives on Education*. Prentice Hall

Hall, Edward T. *The Silent Language*. (1973) Anchor Books Edition

Hamby, B.W. (2007). *The Philosophy of Anything: Critical Thinking in Context*. Dubuque, Iowa. Kendall Hunt Publishing Company.

Hammond, M. & Collins, R. (1991). *Self-directed learning: Critical Practice*. Kogan Page.

Israel, M. & Hay, I. (2006) *Research Ethics for Social Scientists: Between Ethical Conduct and Regulatory Compliance*. London: Sage.

Kotter, John P. (1996) L*eading Change*. Harvard Business School

Leithwood, K. (Ed.) (2000). *Understanding Schools as Intelligent Systems*. CT: JAI Press

Lewin, Kurt, (1948) *Resolving Social Conflicts and Field Theory in Social Science*.

McLuhan, Marshall (1967) *The Medium is the Message*. London: Allen Lane

Miller, James Grier, (1978). *Living Systems*. New York: McGraw-Hill.

O'Toole, James. (1995). *Leading Change: Overcoming the Ideology of Comfort and The Tyranny of Custom*. San Francisco: Jossey-Bass Publishers.

Pohl, Michael. (1999). *Learning to Think, Thinking to Learn: Models and Strategies to Develop a Classroom Culture of Thinking*. Hawker Brownlow Ed.

Reid, Clyde (1967) *The Empty Pulpit*. Harper & Row, New York.

Ruane, Janet. M. (2004). *Essentials of Research Methods: A Guide to Social Science Researc*h. Blackwell.

Schaller, Lyle. (1972). *The Change Agent*. Nashville: Abingdon.

Seech, Zachary (2005), *Open Minds and Everyday Reasoning*, 2nd Edition. Belmont, CA: Wadsworth/Thomson Learning.

Shook, John. (2000). *Dewey's Empirical Theory of Knowledge and Reality*. The Vanderbilt Library of American Philosophy.

Sleeper, R.W. (2001). *The Necessity of Pragmatism: John Dewey's conception of Philosophy*. Introduction by Tom Burke. University of Illinois Press.

Swanson, G.A. & Miller, James Grier. (1989) *Measurement and Interpretation in Accounting: A Living Systems Theory Approach.* New York: Qurum Books.

Swanson, G.A., and Green, Hollis L. (1991, 2004). *Understanding Scientific Research: An Introductory Handbook for the Social Professions.* Nashville: Oxford/ACRSS Press.

White, Alasdair A. K. (2008). *From Comfort Zone to Performance Management.* White & MacLean Publishing.

Wlodkowski, R. J. (1998). *Enhancing Adult Motivation to Learn.* San Francisco, Jossey-Bass Publications.

Online Resources

Online International Journals Research methods knowledge database. *SocialResearchMethods.org*

Resource for methods in evaluation in social research. *gsociology.icaap.org/*

Research methods and statistics arena. *ResearchMethodsArena.com/resources/*

Quantitative and Qualitative Analysis in Social Sciences. *Qass.uk/*

Social Research Update. *sru.soc.surrey.ac.uk/*

Survey Research Methods. *ojs.ub.uni-konstanz.de*

This work is based on

adult involvement in humanitarian and faith-based projects, Civil Rights Movement, Public Service and as a Distinguished Professor of Education and Social Change at the graduate level. Plus traveling and lecturing in over 100 countries.

1. Remind them they must line up under the authority of governments and comply with those in authority, and be willing to do honorable work,

2. they are not to speak injuriously of anyone and avoid quarreling, be gentle and demonstrate a willingness to learn.

3. For we all were once foolish, disobedient, being deceived and serving as slaves to various desires for pleasures, living in hatred and resentment, detestable ourselves and hating each other.

4. Then the kindness and saving love of God was made manifest to all men,

5. it was not by personal works of righteousness that we did that saved us, but His mercy, with the cleansing power of rebirth and restoring of the Holy Spirit;

6. which He poured out in abundance on us through Jesus Christ our Savior;

7. that being declared righteous by His grace, we should be made heirs of eternal life through faith and hopeful expectation.

(Titus 3:1-7 EDNT)

This book is a call to action for faith-based people to strive for constructive social change in the community where they live, work and worship. This must begin with an individual, move to the family, then to groups, then to community and hopefully to a civil society. Many others have written on this subject; *Navigating Multiculturalism* is part of my legacy statement to express personal concern and offer a plan for constructive social change. It will not come in time for this late Octogenarian to personally witness the hopeful change. It may be delayed indefinitely if good people do nothing. ***The outcome may depend on you! Will you accept the challenge?***

www.ingramcontent.com/pod-product-compliance
Lightning Source LLC
Chambersburg PA
CBHW070813270326
41927CB00010B/2403